HOT RODS

HOT RODS

THE HISTORY OF HOT RODS IN 500 PHOTOS

Kev Elliott

CRESTLINE

Library of Congress Cataloging-in-Publication Data Available

ISBN 0-7603-1435-7

Designed and edited by:
FOCUS PUBLISHING, 11a St Botolph's Road, Sevenoaks,
Kent, England TN13 3AJ
Editors: Guy Croton, Vanessa Townsend
Designer: Philip Clucas MSIAD

Salamander editor: Marie Clayton
Salamander publishing director: Colin Gower

Printed and bound in Taiwan

Contents

1

Introduction

Hot rodding has a rich history that only recently has started to be documented. The importance of the early speed pioneers, and the consequences of what they achieved out on the dry lake beds in the Californian desert or at Bonneville Salt Flats, shouldn't be underestimated, as much of today's performance parts industry is directly related to those efforts, with many of those early hot rodders also going on to achieve fame in other forms of motorsport.
But hot rodding is also more than just the cars. It's art, both in the form of the cars and what has been dubbed Kustom Kulture. It's speed and power, talent and skill. Most importantly, it's a way of life.

Left: An ex-*Rod & Custom* magazine car, this 1928 Model A has been a hot rod for most of its life, and remains fairly untouched.

In The Beginning...

Hot rodding is, for want of a better description, the end result of wanting to modify a car to go faster. It's as simple and basic as that, though of course over the years performance hasn't been the only reason for building a hot rod. All over the world people have been pitting their cars against each other since the automobile was invented, but hot rodding was born out on the dry lake beds and deserted highways of southern California as far back as the 1920s. The lake beds are only a few miles north of Los Angeles, and provided the perfect venue for high speed racing, with relatively smooth, flat expanses stretching as far as you could want to stay at full throttle. The other defining factor was the Ford Motor Company—or more specifically the cars produced by that company.

Right: Though hot rodding had been around for a few years, it wasn't until the arrival of *Hot Rod* magazine in 1948 that the hobby had any kind of voice. Other magazines followed, and word spread around the world. Magazines have always been important in setting trends, relaying information, and providing inspiration.

As well as technical articles and feature cars, probably the most important content of magazines, both in the early days and now, is the advertisements. The numerous speed shops and equipment manufacturers soon realized that advertising in the new *Hot Rod* magazine brought them business, and with it the arrival of mail order speed parts.

Above: A timeless picture, and a scene that has remained constant for the past 60 or more years—a hot rodder wrenching on his engine in his driveway. There's huge satisfaction to be had from driving a car you built yourself.

Henry Ford sure made things easy for hot rodders, and it's no surprise his products accounted for virtually all hot rods until the mid-'50s. Even today, Ford bodies are still the predominant marque in the hobby.

With the first widely available V8 engine fitted to '32 Fords—coupled with the ease with which the fenders and running boards could be removed from those cars—the blueprint for the classic Deuce hot rod almost drew itself. The burgeoning performance aftermarket, and appearance of speed shops in southern California fed the rodders' and racers' need for tuning equipment, pretty soon supplying parts by mail order across the country with the introduction of *Hot Rod* magazine in 1948.

This was almost the final piece of the jigsaw, as it provided gearheads nationwide, and even internationally, with an insight to what was happening on the West Coast of America, and turned hot rodding, and street rodding into the global hobby we enjoy today. You may not be able to speak a foreign language, but you'll be able to make yourself understood to a hot rodder whichever country they're from. A cool car is a cool car whatever part of the world you may find yourself in!

Vintage Tin

One of the most important decisions when starting a project is which body style to go for, and what will it be made from. Do you start with a complete car or just a body? Will it be steel or fiberglass?

Hot rods, or street rods as the majority are known as today, may be based

on old cars, but 70 years after the '32 Ford made its debut, there are precious few left—and certainly not many to be had at bargain prices. You'll occasionally hear of a good deal, but any decent steel bodies or complete cars will nowadays command primo prices.

Enter the fiberglass reproduction body manufacturer, and there are many of them, without whom a high percentage of rodders would never be able to build their dream car. These folks have made it possible for countless street rods to be on the street. From the very basic T bucket

bodies offered back in the '60s there is now a huge choice available, from Model Ts, As and Bs through '33 and '41 Willys coupes, Plymouths, Thames, and Anglias, and much more. It's not just coupes and roadsters either, with sedan deliveries, open and closed pick-ups... the list goes on—and that's not counting the huge numbers of panels available, such as fenders and hoods, for more obscure models.

In recent years it has even become possible to purchase brand new steel bodies for Model A, B and '34 roadsters—something no-one dared dream of only a few short years ago. People like Marcel DeLay and Ron Covell have been able to build one-off metal bodies for a number of years, but now companies have tooled up to reproduce early Ford bodies in stock form, so much so that the sheetmetal is interchangeable with genuine items.

The original stuff is still out there though, seemingly more so than ten or 20 years ago. Maybe it's because these days people are prepared to restore a rusty hulk, accepting it may be 50 or more years old, whereas in

Above: All projects have to start somewhere, but perhaps not here, huh? With missing fenders and front sheetmetal, plenty of rust to contend with, and most likely some hefty dings from that chain holding this "unfinished project" onto the trailer, it'd take a determined builder to see this through to a running rod.

years gone by they still expected to be able to find rust-free cars with ease. Maybe it's because these days repair panels for the vast majority of early cars, whether they are Ford, Chevrolet or whatever, are available just a phone call or mouse click away—eliminating all that laborious fabrication. Or maybe it's because not everyone is just after a '32 coupe, and will tackle projects from other marques.

Trawl the swapmeets and there are plenty of steel bodies for sale, even if their age is reflected by their condition. The question that has to be asked is, how badly do you want a steel rod? Of course, the question simply isn't even an option for some, and steel is the only way to go, while for others fiberglass offers an easy answer to sourcing a body.

Below: Not strictly a barn find, this is one of Jeff Beck's collection of '32 Fords, but imagine stumbling across a three window like this. Dry stored for years, you know the body's going to be in great shape.

Opposite: Rusty, dented, and with everything that isn't sheetmetal missing. Not a popular marque either, so you've really got to want one badly to go for this basket case.

Professional Help

Long gone are the days when a hot rod was built entirely at home. Sure, some still like to undertake all the work themselves, some like to handle the assembly or the detailing, and some like to leave the whole build to professionals, occasionally leaving them to make all the decisions—right down to final color choice. Others might have just a rolling chassis built by a shop, while some shop owners encourage the customer to become involved in the project physically, as well as financially.

These shops are important for the hobby, just as their customers are who order ultimately high profile cars. Without them there would be no-one pushing the envelope, encouraging the hobby to take its next step forward.

Left: This '38 Chevy coupe turned roadster was in Sam Foose's shop for a complete makeover, now channeled over a Corvette-suspended tube frame with a Dan Fink-fabricated grille.

Below: Rolling chassis are like works of art, and it's often a shame to cover them with bodies. A '34 coupe body will hide the owner-milled billet A arm front and four bar rear suspensions here.

Opposite: How would you like your '32? A woodie or a roadster? Occupying Barry Lobeck's shop in Ohio in the late '80s was the NSRA giveaway '32 roadster, alongside a neat '32 woodie. The orange roadster was very traditional, with a dropped front axle.

But not all shops build America's Most Beautiful Roadster (AMBR) or Ridler award winning or other high profile cars. Not all shops are owned by big "names" in the hobby. For every Roy Brizio, or Posies, every Boyd Coddington, or Bobby Alloway, there are hundreds of smaller shops building someone's dream hot rod.

From the earliest days of the automobile there have been coachbuilders and craftsmen able to rebody or alter an existing vehicle, and the modern rod shop is not all that far removed from them. But rod shops are not a recent phenomenon, going back to the '40s and '50s with shops such as Valley Custom and Barris Customs, both turning out work on what were the high end cars of their time. Fast forward 50 years and almost every big trophy winner or influential rod is the work of one or more shops.

Possibly the best known shop of recent times is Hot Rods by Boyd. Originating in founder Boyd Coddington's home garage in Cypress, California in 1978, the ultimately publicly-traded company occupied a 140,000 square foot facility, including Boyd's Wheels, a separate company born out of machining billet

Above: No prizes for guessing whose shop this was. That's Boydster II behind Sportstar, which blends styling cues from many sports cars as well as early Fords, packaged in a coachbuilt body that could only come from the pen of a hot rodder—in this case Chip Foose.

Right: Fred Warren's '33 three window takes shape at Boyds. With in-board pushrod operated coilovers, a high-tech drivetrain, and many bodymods including an alligator-style hood, it went beyond the original intention to build an updated version of the Vern Luce coupe for the 1990s.

Below: Could this be the chassis for Chip Foose's rear engined coupe project? That's a hemi and this is at the old Hot Rods by Boyd shop when Foose was working there.

centers for three piece split rim wheels in the 1980s, and turning out over 100,000 CNC machined wheels per year by the 1990s. Boyd's Wheels was a success, but so was the hot rod shop, producing six AMBR winners—Boyd himself the owner of the last one, as well as numerous landmark street rods and customs, some of which are included in this book.

With a reputation quickly gained for building neat rods for himself, and promoting the trend for billet aluminum, cars built by Hot Rods by Boyd had a distinctive "look" that at the beginning elevated them above most of their contemporaries. When Jamie Musselman's Roadster

won the AMBR trophy, critics claimed that the competition had been raised to levels where the backyard builder could no longer compete, but in the years since, the ante has been upped considerably by builders other than Boyd.

While Boyd was busy in southern California, another high profile shop was also building rods in south San Francisco. Roy Brizio Street Rods has been putting together turnkey cars for more than 20 years, with AMBR winners to their credit, as well as a string of dual purpose show-winning driveable cars. Son of Andy Brizio, who operated a rodshop and Champion Speed Shop in the '60s, at the age of 21 Roy opened the doors to his own shop in '76 when his father sold the businesses and started a T shirt

Above: A primered Model A Tudor on Deuce rails undergoes a roof chop. These are one of the easier body styles to chop as the pillars are virtually vertical, making lining up the lowered roof simple.

Opposite: A mixed bunch of just started, in progress, and almost finished cars occupy Roy Brizio's busy shop. The final assembly is on the checkered flooring, with fabrication in the rear of the building.

Left: This 1937 Ford pick-up is coming together at the Limeworks, a Californian shop owned and operated by a British rodder, hence the name with its Limey connection.

printing concern. Having built seven cars in association with Ford Motorsport, and six for Edelbrock, Roy Brizio Street Rods not only has some heavy-hitting corporate clients, but also celebrity customers too, such as Reggie Jackson, Jimmy Vaughn, Jeff Beck, and Eric Clapton. Whether a customer is a celebrity or not though, they all get a "real" hot rod from Brizio, a solid car with expert craftsmanship that can be driven reliably.

Across the country in Tampa, Florida, Hercules Motor Company has been trading since 1976 and specializes in '33 and '34 Ford woodies,

even fabricating their own chassis, as well as new steel cowls and floors. The wooden bodies in both two and four-door versions are fabricated in-house, as are three piece hoods for '32 through '34 Fords. Hercules build both turnkey cars and rolling chassis.

Left: There's a long way to go on this blown and injected Willys coupe, with just an engine, a body, and the beginnings of a chassis on the jig, but employing a competent shop should mean the job gets done quickly.

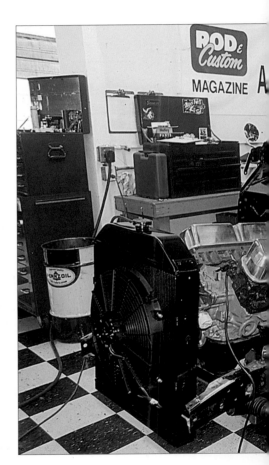

Left: Here's a closer look at the '40 Ford convertible seen in Foy Brizio's shop on page 20. The body looks stock from the outside, but the Brizio crew are updating the running gear using Mustang II independent suspension at the front and working their way through the whole chassis.

Below: The Hercules Motor Car Company produces these '33 and '34 Ford woodies, in both two and four-door configurations, with all new steel cowls, floors and subframes manufactured in-house. Chassis for '32 through '34 Fords are also fabricated at the facility.

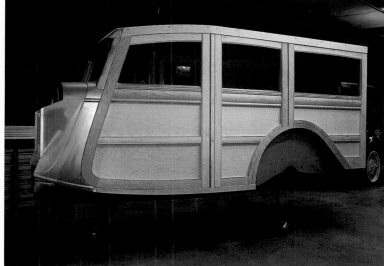

Left: The guys at Hercules have this demo '33/'34 front end to display their talents, as everything seen here comes into the shop as flat steel sheet, before the crew put their skill to work.

Below: Not all projects are shop-built. This '60s style rolling '32 frame was put together in a home garage. The finished rod was built there too, and to the same high standards.

Back across in California, one of So Cal Speed Shop's popular products is the Step-Boxed chassis for '32 and '28 Fords. So Cal Speed Shop is one of the oldest names in the business, though the modern version hasn't traded continuously since Alex Xydias opened the company's doors back in 1946 in Burbank. The speed equipment business underwent many changes, especially after the introduction of OHV V8s in the '50s meant that Ford's flathead V8 wasn't the performance mainstay any longer. Xydias closed the company down in 1961, resurrecting the name in 1997 with Pete Chapouris, ex co-founder of Pete and Jakes Hot Rod Parts, who changed the name of his then-business PC3g, the Pete Chapouris Group, to So Cal Speed Shop.

The company fast gained a reputation for high quality vehicles, its team of craftsmen building many award-winning cars and trucks, as well as restoring vintage hot rods and race cars, some of which went on to appear at the prestigious Pebble Beach Concours D'Elegance. The company has also worked with Ford and Chrysler on project vehicles, developing concepts and products, and building the vehicles.

Above: So Cal Speed Shop tackled the build on this extended cab pick-up, using Kugel Komponents independent suspension at all four corners, meaning occupants are assured of a smooth ride, and extra comfort thanks to the additional legroom provided by the cab stretch.

Below: When Bruce Meyer bought the Bob McGee roadster, originally built in '47, he entrusted So Cal Speed Shop with its restoration to its 1948 guise, when it featured on the cover of *Hot Rod* magazine. Unusual mods for the time were the filled frame horns, and molded and peaked spreader bar, as well as the Z'd '32 frame.

Of course, enlisting professional help during a project doesn't always mean having a complete car built. Many shops will undertake partial builds, completing the work an individual may not have the skills to attempt themselves—such as fabricating and TiG welding a tube chassis or installing chassis crossmembers. With such jobs completed and the parts painted, final assembly is often an enjoyable task that the owner will tackle themselves.

Jobs such as upholstery and paint have always been sub-contracted, so doing the same with other aspects of a build-up should be no different, and with the change in attitudes to pro-built cars, plus the number of pro shops in business, it makes sense and results in a quicker build if professionals are used.

Of course, one aspect of building any car cannot be avoided, and that is where to buy the parts it's constructed from. Most rod shops have parts departments or retail stores where a vast range of parts can be purchased, while some businesses thrive on purely supplying parts with no workshop facilities at all.

CW Moss in Orange, California, is one such store—literally a supermarket crammed with both new and used parts for sale. Whether you're after a grille shell or a complete dashboard for an

Right: Just part of CW Moss' showroom, with display cases showcasing the thousands of products on offer, with larger items like grilles and steering wheels hanging on the walls. If it's early Ford parts that are required, there's not a lot the company's huge inventory doesn't cover.

Left: Under construction, this Pro Street Willys pick-up features interesting front suspension top mounts. The tube frame picks up the McPherson strut tops this way so as not to intrude on the fender line when the sheet metal is in place. Usually this type of car, with a low fender line, would need to run either a tube or beam axle, or independent suspension.

early Ford, you'll most likely find it here, parts in stock ranging from new old stock (NOS) steering wheels to light lenses, rubber pedal covers to kingpin sets. The used parts section is a veritable Aladdin's Cave of treasures to any early Ford fan.

Mooneyes is another store worthy of note—the Moon logo one of the world's most recognizable. Starting his fledgling Moon Automotive business behind the family cafe in Santa Fe Springs with a product line including fuel blocks, foot shaped gas pedals, spun aluminum fuel tanks, and soon, the famous Moon disc, Dean Moon

Above: Another home-built rod, this Willys chassis uses the original frame rails, now boxed, with smaller box section crossmembers which the exhaust and driveshaft pass through. The big-block Chevy is supported by a fatman Fabrications Mustang II-based IFS.

Opposite: Another look at part of CW Moss' impressive store. You'd be forgiven for thinking that you'd stepped into a museum, but hot rodders aren't the company's only clientele, with many restorers relying on their parts service, too.

Left: Mooneyes still occupies the same building in Santa Fe Springs that Dean Moon moved the Moon Equipment Company to in the '50s. The retail store today sells the full range of Moon products, plus much more.

carved himself a niche in the hot rod parts business. At one stage in the '50s, 10,000 Moon discs were sold in a month, the hand-spun discs popular with lakes racers as a cheap way to smooth the aerodynamics of a spinning wheel. With products from other manufacturers added to the range, and a change in company name to Moon Equipment Company, the same premises Moon moved to in the mid-'50s are still occupied by the company today—even though Moon passed away in the late 1980s and his company, now called Mooneyes, is owned by Japanese. The store in Santa Fe Springs still sells the Moon range of products as well as accessories and "kustom kulture" items and literature. Of course, the famous Moon eyes decals are still available!

Bringing Up the Rear

In hot rodding's infancy little thought was given to the rear axle. Engines were tuned for increased power, but with top speed at the lakes being the measure of performance—rather than the later measure of elapsed times at a drag strip—the stresses put on the rear axle were rarely enough to cause damage, as launches were not as vicious, and the tires would break away on the loose surface anyhow. With the advent of drag racing, stronger axles, and quick change third members started showing up. The quickchange enabled a racer to

Below left: About as traditional as it comes, though completely chromed, here's an early Ford axle with a quick change center section.

Below: Still with a quick change, though this time using 9in Ford axles and brakes, ladder bars and Aldan coilovers take care of location and suspension duties.

Right: Using a Jaguar third member, the remainder of this independent suspension system is entirely hand-built, from the billet driveshafts to the tubular control arms. The coilover shocks lie flat above the crossmember, operated by pushrods and cantilevers.

drive to the track at a comfortable engine rpm, swap the gear ratio in a matter of minutes to provide quicker acceleration, then swap back again for the drive home. Of course the quick change bolted into early Ford axles, but by the '50s and '60s stronger axles came into vogue, such as Oldsmobile units in drag cars.

The all-time favorite axle for hot rodders has to be the 9in Ford axle. First introduced in the '50s, the 9in was strong, came in numerous ratios depending on which car it came out of, was relatively cheap, and was easily narrowed. The '70s and '80s brought independent rear suspensions, first with Jaguar and Corvette axles, then later with aftermarket set-ups, culminating in the works of art seen under the rear of rods from shops such as Hot Rods by Boyd. For strength though, a ive axle will always be best, so it should come as no surprise that although Ford no longer produces the 9in, aftermarket versions are still very much in demand.

Museums and Collections

It has only been in recent years that hot rodding has gained what might be termed respectability. In the hobby's early years, anyone calling themselves a hot rodder had a reputation as a troublemaker, and an illegal street racer before they were given a chance to prove otherwise, an image not helped by Hollywood's B movies, which nearly always depicted hot rodders badly.

While it may have been a "cool" image that a few youngsters aspired to, it didn't help the public's perception of the hobby at all. Never mind the fact that hot rodders went on to participate in, and build and tune cars for Indianapolis, construct all-time great sports cars such as the Shelby Cobra, set world land speed records, and other great achievements, they would always be perceived as reckless youths riding around in dangerous, hopped-up jalopies.

Below: Swede Sven Sandberg built this '32 five window in '58, sold it in the '70s, and bought it back to restore in the '90s—a big-block Chevy replacing the Rocket 88 mill originally used.

Above: In the foreground we see possibly the most famous gasser of them all—the Stone, Woods and Cook '41 Willys. Meanwhile, examine the differences between a stock '33 and a KS Pitman's chopped, lowered, and stretched drag coupe.

Right: Pure Hell and Pure Heaven, similar Fuel Altereds but given completely opposite names. In 1968 Rich Guasco's Pure Hell set the NHRA AA/FA record at 7.68/208.80mph using a blown and injected Chrysler hemi engine. A previous version which crashed in '67 had been powered by a small-block Chevy motor.

It was this very reasoning that prompted the change in the 1970s from calling this pastime "hot rodding" to referring to it as "street rodding."

Followers and participants of other forms of auto-related hobbies and motorsports have long since been collecting and restoring significant cars from their past, but it's only recently that hot rodders have started doing the same.

It's taken the actions of a few clued-up individuals to make others see that these cars are important

Above: A 214ci Model B motor fitted with a riley four port cylinder head powered this CRA track roadster, driven by Rosie Roussel.

Right: John Athan's '29 Ford roadster was driven by Elvis Presley in the movie, *Loving You*. Dual carbs and outside exhausts prettied-up the flathead, along with a unique homemade windshield.

historically, and sometimes force changes to existing events to make them accept hot rods or vintage dragsters as legitimate cars of historic importance.

Amazingly there are a great many landmark cars still in existence from hot rodding, lakes racing, and drag racing, and others, either restored or in original condition, are on loan to museums for the rest of us to enjoy. The NHRA Motorsports Museum near the Pomona dragstrip in

California is home to such vehicles that would otherwise be kept away from public view, illustrating the history of hot rodding and drag racing from its roots to today's 300mph sport. The 60-odd exhibits comprise cars that have been restored and donated, or on loan for extended periods.

Below: Built and driven by Art Chrisman, this '31 Ford Model A-bodied chopped coupe was a 200mph record holder at Bonneville, thanks to its 354ci fuel injected Chrysler hemi. Heavily chopped, the windshield aperture was raised into the roof to retain the legally required glass height.

Similar is the Petersen Museum in Los Angeles, containing many historically significant hot rods alongside classic automobiles, again some on loan. Over 150 exhibits on four floors form permanent and changing displays, depicting the evolution of a culture that has influenced life in southern California and particularly in Los Angeles—a city that grew up with the evolution of the car. Though there are always hot

Below: Eddie Miller Jnr's Class B Lakester seen today safe in storage. Powered, unusually by a 248ci Pontiac six cylinder, Miller fabricated his own head and manifold, running a best time of 156mph in '52. The car also made the cover of *Hot Rod* magazine.

Below right: How many private collections like this, hidden from public view, must there be? At least the cars are stored safely, with the chance that maybe one day they'll come out of hibernation. Note the collection of parts on the shelves, too.

rod displays in the museum, it covers the full history of the automobile, with dioramas and exhibition galleries.

Florida is home to Don Garlits' Museum of Drag Racing, housing many important race cars from the sport's past, and not just Garlits' own dragsters but many others on loan from their owners around the country. With 50,000 square feet of display space currently, the museum is constantly growing and changing, now double the size it was when it opened in 1986.

For a few years now the Pebble Beach Concours D'Elegance has accepted hot rods, as has the AACA National Fall Meet at Hershey, where vintage hot rods and drag cars can now legitimately compete in the race car class. However, this certainly hasn't always been the case and it is still something of an uphill struggle at other venues, even with these prestigious events setting somewhat of a precedent.

Of course, many hot rodders are pack rats with private collections of not just old cars but car parts, too. Not all of them want to show their

Below: Down in Memphis. Jim Dodd's eclectic collection contains this Model A roadster pick-up with extended body, aluminum track nose, and tilt bed. Rolling on kidney bean Halibrands and with a high level exhaust, it's just part of a collection that includes Allards, Corvettes, single seat racers, muscle cars, and hot rods.

Right: Jeff Beck has an enviable collection of '32 Fords at home in England, some of which are drivers and some not. Though most have been shipped over from the States, some are found locally too. This chopped Deuce runs a dropped and drilled original I beam.

Below: The Don Garlits Museum of Drag Racing in Florida contains not just famous and historic dragsters, but many of Garlits' own cars as he's a collector of classic vehicles, as well as a renowned drag racer.

Below: Waiting patiently in a wooden-floored building on Jeff Beck's property for their turn to come around again are the Super Prune chopped sedan he's owned since the '70s and a replica of the American Graffiti coupe.

collections to the outside world, and there are even cases of historic and famous old rods being bricked up inside rooms for only the owner to enjoy, or stored in hermetically sealed rooms. Some live in warehouses with others of their ilk, or in private collections in purpose-built buildings. Some may never get to be restored, the owners intending to get around to it "one day." But at least these cars are in safe hands and not rotting away behind a barn somewhere, as is all too often the case.

One man who has been instrumental in hot rodding becoming accepted within the larger scheme of automotive interests is Bruce Meyer. It was he who bought and had So Cal Speed Shop restore the Pierson brothers' famous chopped 2D '34 Ford coupe, as well as the Doane Spencer '32 roadster and other early rods. A peek into Meyer's garage is like peering into a museum, packed as it is with automobilia, pedal cars, trophies, pictures, signs, and associated old clothing, in addition to cars.

The cars range from '32 Fords to a Cobra and Porsche, Ferrari, a Bugatti, and the 1960 Cunningham Le Mans Corvette, but Meyer believes in driving his cars, and isn't afraid to take the Spencer '32 for a drive around Beverley Hills or even further afield. It may be a unique piece of hot rod history—but it's still a car!

Another who believes in driving his collection is musician Jeff Beck. The majority of his cars are '32 Fords, though over the years there have been Model Ts and a hammered '34 coupe. Living in England, the majority of Beck's collection is housed at his centuries-old house, most having been shipped over from California, though he does keep cars there, too, for use when in the States. Though he's been a customer of Roy Brizio's for years, Beck works on his cars himself to a great degree and can occasionally be seen driving his latest creation at the bigger rod runs in England.

Opposite: Hmm, which will it be today, the chopped three window or five window? Life must be tough!

Below: With license tags that read SHE'S A 34, this hammered coupe marks one of Beck's departures from '32 ownership.

Engines

The very heart of any hot rod is the engine. Without a motor, a car is nothing, though unlike most forms of motorsport a hot rod engine is much more than just the powerhouse, as its appearance is usually just as important as the power it produces. Why else would most hot rods run either without a hood or hood sides if not to show off the engine?

In some instances the looks come before the primary function of the motor, using parts that may look great but don't particularly help the engine run well. It's all down to image sometimes. For instance if triple carbs on a small block worked well, wouldn't drag racers the world over be using them?

Above: Supercharged, or blown, and with Ardun heads, this is one impressive flathead. Those heads, named after inventor Zora Arkus Duntov, convert the sidevalve V8 to overhead valve.

Opposite: With much pinstriping and a tribute to Von Dutch and Ed Roth on the firewall, the tri-power-equipped fully dressed Chevy in this '40 Ford is the crowning touch.

Left: With a Hilborn scoop rising high on a polished tunnel ram intake, this small-block Chevy, or "mouse" motor packs a punch in a lightweight T bucket.

Right: San Antonio, Texas, must have felt Eddie Anderson's Bowers magnesium blower-equipped 492ci hemi-motored stretched street T bucket whenever it fired up. With Keith Black Fuel heads, the zoomie headers contained VW baffles, which can't have done much to silence the beast.

Below: The mighty 426ci Chrysler hemi was the engine of choice for many drag racers in the '60s and '70s, but this one's on the street in a T bucket. Twin Dominator carbs sit atop a Roots-type blower—making for an impressive motor.

No, they go for a single four barrel carb in most instances as that works best for performance, but on a nostalgic or period car, nothing beats a tri-power for looks. Well, except a blower maybe, but even then a nostalgia car would need a SCoT or Italmechanicca blower, not a GMC supercharger.

Why? Because it wouldn't look right. If a rod is being built to the style of a particular era, it makes sense to only use parts that were available in that era.

One thing that is pretty mandatory, though, is that hot rods should be powered by a V8.

Right: The heartbeat of Lady Luck II began with a '74 high performance Chevrolet 454 big-block that was bored to 460in³, filled with plenty of go-fast goodies from Comp Cams and Keith Black, and dynoed to the tune of 465bhp and 512lb of torque.

Left: A 396ci big block Chevy, known as a "rat" motor, as the small block is a "mouse," this wears a Holley carb on a same-make Street Dominator intake, with Mickey Thompson valve covers.

Below: The original Dick Flint A had a '40 Merc flathead, but this replica uses a '57 'vette 283 with a Duntov cam and Chevy dual-quad induction for reliability.

There was a time when alternative powerplants were considered, mainly during the gas crisis of the 1970s, with V6s and four bangers making their way into rods, but they just can't cut it in the looks department—or, for that matter, in almost all cases, in terms of performance either. Vintage four bangers have their place in very early style rods, again because that's what was used back then, or in little cars such as T Modifieds, where the space constraints of a full hood make the choice of a V8 virtually impossible, but especially with open engined rods, the symmetry of a V8 is needed to balance the car.

Below: Very common in modern day street rods, new "crate" small-block Chevy engines are available in a selection of sizes and horsepower ratings. Being able to order a new motor direct from the local dealer makes things easy.

If you've ever seen a straight six-motored rod you'll have noticed the bank of exhaust pipes on one side, with nothing to balance them on the other—unless there's a pretty trick bank of carbs there to even things up, though usually the carbs are sited on the same side of the engine as the exhaust. The sheer size of a V8 fills the engine bay too, but it's the performance they give that is their main reason for being transplanted into little old cars.

There's an equation that goes something like "small car plus big engine equals more power," and it's certainly true with hot rods. After all, they originally came about to satisfy their owners' greed for speed, and by their very nature are supposed to be fast machines.

In the very early days of hot rodding the choice was pretty much limited to Ford Model T and Chevy four bangers, with a small backyard speed parts industry supporting these engines. Then Ford introduced its flathead V8 in 1932 and suddenly everything else fell by the wayside. Performance parts quickly became available for this new record setting engine—indeed, many of today's speed equipment manufacturers started by making parts for the flathead. It was the engine to have for the next 20 years, until the introduction of overhead valve engines.

Overhead conversions had been available for the flathead for years—the most famous being the Ardun conversion—and the four cylinder motors before it. But engines such

Below: Three Holley 94s on an Offenhauser intake feed this 270ci '55 Dodge Red Ram hemi in a '34 Dodge pick-up. Note the coil which has been sunk into the firewall, making a neat feature of a necessary component.

as Chrysler's hemi, and Oldsmobile, Studebaker, Buick, Pontiac, and Cadillac OHV V8s suddenly eclipsed the faithful flathead and appeared in all sorts of rods—both on the street, and at the lakes and drags.

Probably the most popular hot rod engine of them all, the small-block Chevy, saw the light of day in 1955, with a displacement of 265 cubic inches, and proceeded to

Above: Dual Stromberg 97s on a Marshall supercharger wake up this 24 stud flathead, helped by Harrell finned aluminum heads and an Iskendarian 7/ race camshaft. A Vertex magneto lights the fire—the only thing telling you this isn't a vintage set-up is the alternator.

Left: Straight six engines have their devotees and even their own clubs. Set up right these motors produce a distinct sound of their own that is as appealing to those who love them as the sound of a V8 to most others. With three carbs and a six branch header, this six pot is a screamer.

Left: This 1946 59AB flathead uses a 4in stroke Mercury crank, and oversize Jahns pistons to displace 284ci. An Isky 400Jnr cam, polished Navarro heads, and two Stromberg 97s on a Tattersfield manifold help it run as good as it looks.

Opposite bottom: The four banger in this Model A runs a Donningham overhead valve conversion, twin carbs, a lakes style header, and a modern alternator.

Below: A Tri-power and finned centre bolt Offenhauser valve covers lend a vintage feel here, especially with the plain chrome air cleaners.

grow in size until it reached 350ci and beyond, becoming the basis for hot rods and drag cars even today. Ford itself abandoned the flathead in 1954, though the engines were still in production until fairly recently—and in Europe until the early 1990s they were used as pump engines and military hardware!

The aftermarket parts industry that has grown up with hot rodding is now a multi-million dollar industry,

providing every part you could possibly think of for all manner of engines. Even aftermarket aluminum blocks became available in the early 1970s and today, most of the major OEM manufacturers offer performance "crate motors" from their own inventory, recognizing the hot rodder's need for speed—and speed not just in performance, but in buying engines that can be ordered simply by calling a local dealer and quoting a part number.

It's all a far cry from the early days of the 1940s when the likes of Weiand, Offenhauser, and Edelbrock first cast their high compression cylinder heads for flathead V8s, or even further back with Winfield, Miller, Rajo Roof, or Riley hop up parts for Ford T, A and B models. Those early days of hot rodding spawned most of the performance equipment available today, and most of those companies were started by young hot rodders.

One of the most visual additions that can be made to an engine is the induction set-up. Even internally stock engines can look great with a set of aluminum valve covers, headers, and a neat induction package.

The sky's the limit too, quite literally with the height of some induction systems! Whether it's a single carb, two, three, four, five on some straight sixes, or even six, intake manifolds are available for most motors to suit. Then there's tunnel rams, polished or unpolished, single or twin carb, high rise manifolds, single plane or dual plane, cross ram—take your pick.

Fancy a blower? Fine, will it be a GMC 4-71, 6-71, 8-71 or larger? Or how about a SCoT, B&M, Shorrocks, Wade, Mooneyham, BDS, McCullough? The list is seemingly endless, as is the number, size, and type of engine. And then there's fuel injection to consider. While hot rod engines can still be built simply, with a distributor that contains points and a rotor arm, and a carburetor, modern electronics has made massive inroads into the hobby, with fuel injection systems that can now be programed using a laptop computer, and mapped according to the operator's wishes. Injection no longer means the leaky and unreliable components of yesterday, but all the advantages of modern componentry, polished and looking great, of course!

Above: Blown flatheads are nothing new, but seeing a blower this size on Henry's finest is a bit of a surprise, especially with twin Holley carbs on top—definitely a case of over-induction!

Opposite: With velocity stacks just poking out the top of the engine bay on this '32, everything on the big-block Ford motor is either polished or chromed, including the hoses. A stainless steel firewall makes it even brighter.

Interiors and Dashes

Of course, performance engines require not just looking after, but need to offer feedback to the driver, which is where gauges and dashboards come in. Hot rodders have always liked going fast, yet at the same time most tried to make their rod appear different. The addition of a dash panel from an upmarket marque has always been a neat way of improving a car, as it invariably offers a selection of gauges with which to monitor the engine's internal condition.

A perennial favourite with rodders is the Auburn dash, a very popular addition in the '40s, making the dash worth as much as a whole '31-'33 Auburn at the time. Other high end dashes were always admired, and sometimes even complete dashes would be swapped from one model to another—for instance, a complete '40 Ford dash, from door pillar to door pillar, would be made to fit a '32 roadster, offering a completely different look to the earlier car's interior. The steering column and 'wheel from a '40 was also a popular swap into the earlier Fords, as it offered a column shifter, meaning three people could be squeezed into the confines of a '32 or '34 in comfort. Of course, this meant changing the transmission to a side shift model at the same time, as the column shifter would not hook up to a floor shift trans.

As hot rods became more refined and were not just used for flying across dry lake beds at high speed, so their interiors began to become more comfortable.

Above: An Auburn dash with early Stewart Warner gauges sits well in the replica Dick Flint roadster with a Bell four-spoke 'wheel. Note how little interior space there is when a Model A roadster body is channeled over the frame.

Right: Barney Navarro's old T, now owned by Scott Perrot, features a dash signed by the original builder after its restoration. The Bell 'wheel connects to a sprint car box. The hand pump on the right is used to boost fuel pressure.

Tuck 'n' roll upholstery, carpets, headliners, and full width custom dashes filled with desirable Stewart Warner gauges all became the norm rather than the exception, along with chromed parts, pinstriping, and detailing.

Modern street rod interiors today will most likely include air conditioning, heaters, electric windows, and stereo systems, along with digital instruments, electric and heated seats, sculptured upholstery, and more. In fact, anything that's available in a new car will have been

Above: The early dash panel in this '32 Ford roadster contains enough gauges to relay all vital information to the driver. Apart from the dash and the three-spoke 'wheel, the rest of the interior is fairly stock '32, from the shifter on the top loader trans to the pedals. A re-trim in brown leather and matching carpet modernizes it somewhat.

Right: The machine-turned dash in this all-aluminum replica '28 A roadster contains Stewart Warner gauges, as any self-respecting early style rod should—though there's precious little in the way of creature comforts apart from a couple of minimally padded seats and aluminum shields over the exhaust, which runs inside the car above the belly pan.

installed in a street rod somewhere. The basic creature comforts of a Mexican blanket thrown over torn upholstery that sufficed decades ago has today been superseded by leather, Naugahyde, tweed, alcantra, and other exotic materials to produce unique interiors that wouldn't look out of place in luxury cars.

Even the humble steering wheel hasn't escaped. Where once it was the height of cool to have a '40 Ford wheel or three or four-spoke Bell 'wheel in a rod, today billet 'wheels are the trend—thankfully these days leather trimmed or half trimmed, though when billet aluminum hit the scene big time in the '80s there were many rods running bare billet steering wheels, including the rim. Some companies, such as LeCarra, offer aftermarket 'wheels that look like 1950s versions, except in much smaller diameters. Ironically, the upsurge of interest in nostalgia rods has meant that the actual originals are now in demand again.

Right: We'd guess this '40 Ford is called the Wanderer judging by the dash! Plenty of pinstriping adorns what is essentially a stock dash with additional gauges. White tuck 'n' roll contrasts nicely with the white edged black carpet.

Left: It's got the appearance of an old interior at first glance, but note the molded door and kick panels, with speaker holes in the door, the color-matched steering wheel, the tach mount and column drop, and the finish on the dash.

Below: Not all hot rod interiors are luxurious. Mike Callan's Pro Street but race-legal Anglia features aluminum panelling and Autometer gauges once the rollcage has been negotiated.

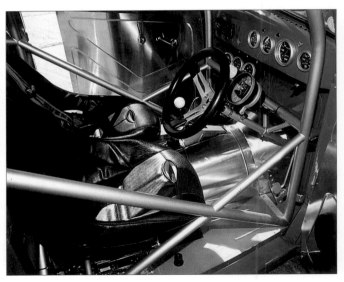

Above: Chuck de Heras' '40 Ford sports a 10in narrowed '55 T bird dash and '57 Fairlane 'wheel, white and orange vinyl tuck 'n' roll on a Glide Engineering bench seat, and chromed window garnish moldings.

Right: Tommy Ivo's T bucket featured a full width dash made by Ivo from tubing and sheet metal, holding Stewart Warner gauges, an eight ball topped the extended shifter and a three-spoke Bell 'wheel sat atop the near-vertical chromed column.

Tot Rods, Toys and Collectables

A question currently on many peoples lips is where the next generation of hot rodders is going to come from. The nostalgia rod scene has brought many young adults to the hobby, but how about these "tot rods" for children? If there's one thing guaranteed to get a kid's attention it has to be these miniature rods that they can drive. Powered by anything from an electric wheelchair motor, through to automatic moped engines and lawnmower motors to full size motorcycle engines, tot rods are great for kids as it gets them involved, helps them learn the mechanical basics, and can be built to go as fast or slow as the parent wishes.

Some rod runs even organize scaled down drag racing for tot rods, though the cars run on their own against the clock for safety reasons. Kids are catered for at the drags too, with a class called Junior Dragster, which allows them to race scaled down rear engined dragsters powered by tuned Briggs and Stratton motors.

Commercially available tot rod bodies can be had in scale '32, '34 and '37 Ford roadster shapes, as well as

Above: With a 90cc automatic moped motor disguised in the front of this hand-built mini-T bucket, it can probably get up a fair turn of speed. There's plenty of work here, from the dropped tube axle to the body and pick-up bed.

Opposite: Start 'em young! Tot rod drag racing for kids is popular at some rod runs. Note the DuVall screen, rollbar, and bumpers on this baby '32 roadster.

Austin J40, with a full complement of necessary hard parts such as chassis, wheels, tires, axles, and so on, though handbuilt tot rods are fairly commonplace—some representing real cars more accurately than others.

Of course, as with the real thing, some builders get carried away, and produce stunning works of art that feature hand-crafted independent suspension systems, wild interiors, one-off aluminum bodies, working differentials, lights and gauges, billet wheels, candy paint jobs, and more. Just as with the real world of show cars, there is always someone pushing the envelope just that

Above: With full fenders and a roof added to convert this '34 into a coupe, wouldn't you have liked to drive this around your neighborhood as a kid?

Opposite: This little Model A roadster pick-up was scratch-built, including the '32-style frame, to replicate the full size truck behind it. The bed is slightly out of proportion as it had to contain the electric motor and battery.

Right: The detailing on this mini-'34 is amazing. For starters a full set of fenders have been added to the commercially available body, with an electric motor fitted in the trunk despite the bug catcher poking through the hood. Wheelie bars add to the effect, and check out that license plate—Boyed!

little bit further. How long will it be until a tot rod is registered for road use or features a working scaled-down V8?

While tot rods appeal to family-oriented rodders, they aren't the only "toys" hot rodders are interested in, with many other hot rod and auto-related items becoming very collectable or becoming a fad. In the '80s valve cover racing was popular at rod runs, where a usually stock pressed steel cover (used for its light weight) had a set of wheels added, and would be gravity raced against another on a sloping track. This again escalated quickly to the point where many valve covers were equipped with super lightweight

Left: L'il Grape is a gasser-style tot rod based on a J40 Austin body. These were originally built as pressed steel pedal car versions of Austin's A40 cars by disabled workers in England— originals today are worth big money. Fiberglass replicas are now available.

Above: Billet independent suspension front and rear, one-off billet wheels, and a working differential and stereo are just some of the tricks on Jonathan Sutherland's hand-built Shockwave-inspired tot rod.

Above right: One-off models such as this turtle-deck track T are very collectable, and a great talking point for any den or living room.

aluminum and carbon fiber wheels, were modified for streamlining and other tricks to make them faster.

The collectable side of hot rodding doesn't stop with owning more than one car, as collecting toys or automobilia such as vintage gas pumps and oil cans is also big news. Anything old is always desirable, but collecting other cars powered by little two stroke motors, model cars, sculptures, artwork, and paintings is also popular. Even old magazines have their devotees, scouring swapmeets for that elusive issue to complete a collection.

Left: Hot rod related collectables range from car parts such as collections of every aftermarket aluminum cylinder head ever manufactured for flathead V8s to artwork, paintings, and pieces such as this "HOT ROD VOODOO PAPA." What has lately been termed Kustom Kulture is hugely collectable with a certain number of hot rodders.

Right: These roughly half-scale "rods" are designed for adults to drive, which seems to somewhat defeat the object when they have a T bucket to cruise in, and don't bear any resemblance to any particular make or model. Bet they're fun though, which is what it's supposed to be all about!

Replicas

With the great interest in finding, restoring or simply owning classic hot rods from the hobby's past at an all-time high, it stands to reason that only one person can own each car at one time and may not wish to sell, or there are cars that no longer exist and so cannot be bought.

This has led to the recreation of famous rods in recent times. Sometimes the original may be altered beyond recognition, yet the replica will stay true to the original build; sometimes the replica will look accurate on the outside, yet employ modern running gear or a different engine to the original. However they're done, when a replica of a car that no longer exists is built, it gives hot rodders a chance to appreciate that car for a second time.

Opposite: This clone of Norm Grabowski's original Kookie car is named Deja Vu and owned by Grant Pendergraft of Oregon. The '62 Cadillac 390ci V8 is backed by a TH400 instead of a '39 Ford toploader though, and the front brakes and exhausts are different from the original.

Right: Jim Busby owns this clone of the famous Dick Flint '29 roadster. There's a twin four barrel-fed 283 Chevy V8 under the hood instead of the '40 Merc flathead the original car runs. The famous '52 *Hot Rod* magazine cover picture is recreated here.

Personal Choices

Hot rodding is a very personal thing as it involves an individual's personal tastes and preferences. A hot rod should only ever be built to please the builder, or owner if a professional shop is handling the build. Though trends come and go, and fashion and peer pressure affect decisions during a project, if the finished car doesn't please the owner, they're not going to enjoy it to the full.

Having said that, for a hobby that shouldn't have any rules, there are many unwritten ones, the parameters of which should be kept to if the finished car is to be accepted by fellow rodders. By way of an example, you wouldn't fit billet aluminum wheels with rubber band tires to the rod on the left, as it wouldn't suit the early theme. With so many styles or rod available to build, whichever one is chosen should be adhered to throughout.

Left: Dave Lukkari's Ardun-motored Model A certainly struck out on its own when built, as the nostalgia movement had yet to get into its stride, yet it was what Dave wanted—and if the lack of paint or the use of early parts offended others, who cared?

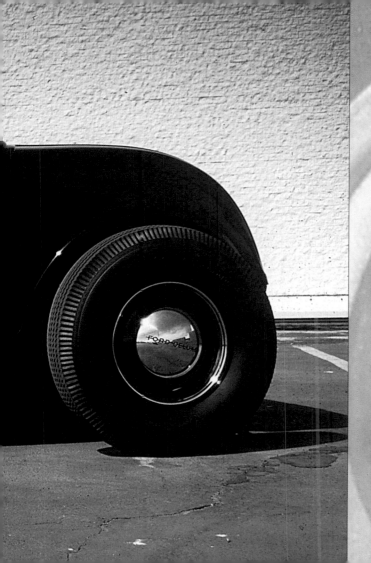

2

1950s

The 1940s and '50s produced what we now regard as some of the most historically important hot rods, and not just from the West Coast either. With the birth of *Hot Rod* magazine to spread the word, and major awards to aim for at shows like the Oakland Roadster Show and Detroit Autorama, the hobby's popularity exploded. Dry lakes racing was an important part of hot rodding back then, with most rods being daily transportation during the week, then driven out to the lakes and stripped for racing on weekends. With virtually all rods powered by Ford's Flathead V8 up until the mid-'50s, competition was fierce, both between individuals and car clubs.

Left: Doane Spencer's Deuce is possibly the quintessential hot rod—a "stripped down" '32 roadster with a flathead V8.

Left: The So Cal Speed Shop belly tank is powered by a flathead V8 fed by four carbs, mounted behind the driver. Using engines of varying displacements, the car achieved records at El Mirage and Bonneville, with an ultimate top speed of 195mph to this approximate length.

Right: Tom Beatty's belly tank was originally fitted with a supercharged Ford flathead, taking it to a top speed of 211.5mph in 1955, though later with an Oldsmobile motor it reached 247mph. It is seen here, in original condition, in 2000.

Opposite: Alex Xydias with his legendary So Cal Speed Shop belly tank. The lakester was formed from a 315 gallon P-38 aircraft auxiliary droppable fuel tank and was one of many lakes racing cars Alex built to promote his speed shop business immediately after World War Two.

Below: "Big Daddy" Don Garlits recreated his first race car, now on display in his drag racing museum in Florida. The Ford flathead-motored modified Model T features a basic rollbar, and was used to tow Garlits' Swamp Rat dragster at nostalgia races for a while.

Above: This 1927 Model T was racing at the lakes in the late 1940s, and appeared at the first Oakland Roadster Show in 1949, as well as at the anniversary show 50 years later.

Left: The Art Chrisman/LeRoy Neumayer car was built using 1928 Chevy framerails, a Franklin front axle and steering, and a Ford Model A rear axle. The first car to run at the inaugural NHRA Nationals in 1955, it was powered by a 304ci Merc motor.

Classic Profile: NEIKAMP ROADSTER

Bill Neikamp's Model A roadster holds an important place in hot rod history, as it was the first winner of the America's Most Beautiful Roadster trophy, at the first Oakland Roadster Show. Built with a $2,000 budget, this was a big buck car for its time, and state of the art with a full belly pan and track nose. Today the car has been fully restored by Jim 'Jake' Jacobs, of Pete & Jakes fame.

Right: Very much styled after circle track racers of the time, the roadster sits low and level, with an aluminum track nose and belly pan. A '37 Ford tube axle graces the front end, with telescopic shocks and '40 hydraulic brakes The chrome nerf bar is also circle track influenced.

Right: The Mercury flatmotor is backed by a '39 transmission, Neikamp recording a speed of 142mph in 1952 at El Mirage dry lake. Over the years the roadster has seen numerous engines, including a nailhead Buick, and small-block Chevy, but a flathead once again occupies the engine bay after a thorough restoration.

Below: With the belly pan extending the full length of the body, the exhausts exit through the rear pan. Jacobs' restoration included having tonneau cover made for the cockpit. Steel wheels adorned with hubcaps and beauty rings became standard fitment on hot rods in the 50s, as the popularity of wire wheels waned with their introduction.

Above: Rico Squaglia built his turtledeck T in 1949, winning the America's Most Beautiful Roadster trophy in 1951. The car subsequently changed hands and was disassembled in the '60s, before Carter Fisher bought it in pieces and undertook its restoration. Nerf bar, hairpin radius rods locating the axles front and rear, as well as a bellypan formed to follow the shape of the lower body, all point to circle track influences.

Left: Famous camshaft grinder Ed Iskenderian built this Model T in 1940, using a '32 Ford engine with Maxi Overhead conversion topped with engraved valve covers featuring his surname. The car was featured on the May 1948 cover of *Hot Rod* magazine.

Below: This 1939 Ford ragtop qualifies as both rod and custom. Modifications include a chopped top, running board removal, the grille swapped for a Chevy item, a de-trim, and all-round suspension lowering.

Left: A Hot Rod cover car in '48, Bob McGee's '32 featured some innovative mode for its time, such as the three piece aluminum hood, hidden hinges, and extended decklid. It later appeared in movies and on TV, and reached 167mph at Bonneville, before current owner Bruce Meyer had it restored to its 1947 configuration.

Opposite: Another AMBR title winner, in '53 this '27T was owned by Dick Williams. It has been restored, though wider rear wheels have been added, and it's now owned by Blackie Gejeian.

Right: Frank Mack won the 1952 Detroit Autorama with this '27T. 1927 Jordan headlights and brass spinners on Hudson caps help it stand out. Unrestored, the T is in fantastic condition, and made an appearance at the 50th Autorama in 2002.

Classic Profile: DICK FLINT ROADSTER

Dick Flint was a college student in 1952 when his daily driven Model A roadster was voted *Hot Rod* magazine's Hot Rod of the Month. Valley Custom carried out the body modifications, including a handformed hood, belly pan, and that distinctive nose and grille, while the dash used an Auburn instrument panel. With a 6in channelled body and Z'd frame, the car sat very low. The styling was much copied at the time, and even today the Flint roadster is admired so much it has been cloned!

The original underwent a total restoration and took top honors in the hot rod class at the 1999 Pebble Beach Concours. This wasn't its first show win either, as it emerged victorious at the Oakland Roadster Show in '51, as well as the Detroit Autorama. Nor was the roadster a slouch at the lakes: it ran 143 in 1950 and 155 in the 1970s.

Right: With a nerf bar protecting the one-off nose, there's a matching nerf bar on the rear of the roadster, incorporating '39 teardrop lights.

Right: Dick used a 1940 Mercury V8 with Edelbrock heads, a Winfield cam, and three carbs when he put the roadster together. After restoration it retained its winning ways, with a First in Class for owner Don Orosco at the Goodwood Festival of Speed in England in 2000.

Below: The Shish Kabob Special was built by Blackie Gejeian in the late '40s, and was street driven and raced before winning the AMBR trophy in '55. The '26T cowl and handbuilt body were leaded to the chassis. The car got its name because Blackie and friends would turn the car on its side at shows every hour to show off the chromed undercarriage!

Above: Michigan's Tommy Foster put this '32 together in 1950, using brand new parts! Double whitewalled motorcycle tires were used up front, and in 1952 a then-new Caddy motor replaced a 59AB flathead.

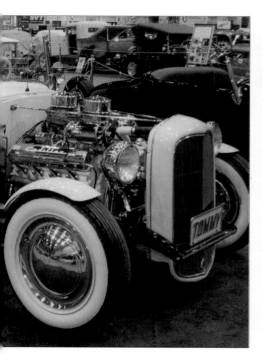

Right: Movie fans may recognise this as the '32 from *Hot Rod Girl*. Its full-house flathead breathes through a pair of 97s on an Evans manifold, with Sharp heads. The lacquer may be a little cracked these days, but it's the real deal.

Below: The Pacific Gunsight Company '32 was originally built in 1946 by Mark McKinney, running 124mph at Bonneville by the 1950s, thanks to a 244ci flathead, '40 Ford trans with Lincoln Zephyr gears, and a Halibrand quick change. Pleasanton's James Palmer has owned this beauty since 1972.

Above: Joe Conforth's '50s-built '28/'29 Ford A pick-up runs an Offy tri-power fed early small-block Chevy linked to a Halibrand quick change axle, all mounted on '32 framerails.

Opposite: A milestone in East Coast rodding history, Fred Steele put this 6in channeled '32 together in 1951 at the age of just 16. The bored and stroked full race flathead feeds a Columbia two speed axle, while that purple is a custom mixed shade. Oh, and Fred still owns it today!

Left: 1950s hot rods are right back in vogue today, and nothing says 1950s more than a deep burgundy Deuce roadster on whitewalls with a full house flathead.

Opposite: Sebastian "Sabie" Rubbo channeled this '36 Ford roadster a massive 6in back in 1946, adding a custom front end with a '37 Ford truck grille, and installing a heavily modified '48 Mercury flathead. Over the years Sabie lived up to his beliefs of driving his car, accruing over 450,000 miles. Present owner Lenny Biondi painstakingly restored the roadster.

Classic Profile: DOANE SPENCER DEUCE

Here's a hot rod that's been everywhere and done everything! Owner and builder Doane Spencer toured 42 states in the car, raced it at the dry lakes and completely rebuilt it to enter the Mexican Road Race, including Z'ding the front and rear of the frame, though the race was banned before the car was finished. Subsequent owner Neal East rebuilt it with a 284ci flathead and drove the wheels off it, even competing in historic road races. It was then stripped for a proper restoration and sold, in pieces, before Bruce Meyer had it restored to Doane Spencer's original specification.

So sought after nowadays, the DuVall screen was one of a batch made for a high school project by George DuVall and donated to Doane's '32.

Right: The pitman arm halfway up the cowl connects to a Schroeder circle track steering box, seen here inside. A full complement of Stewart Warner gauges sit in an engine turned dash, while wipers were fitted to the roadster by Doane as he often ventured far from the West Coast.

Right: The chassis restored to Doane's original specification. The axle was moved in front of the crossmember, which meant that once the frame horns were removed the car could sit lower without using a dropped axle.

Left: Ray Brown used his '32 as daily transport to and from his job at Eddie Meyer's speed equipment company after World War Two, but come the weekend and he could be found at El Mirage, with the headlights and screen removed, racing on the lake bed.

Opposite: L'il Beauty, a 5^1/$_2$in channeled '40 Ford sedan, was built in 1955. The hood was sectioned a like amount before the Barris' Kustom City flared and molded the fenders, and added '57 Lincoln headlights and nerf bars.

Left: Allegedly the first lakes car successfully equipped with a GMC Roots-type supercharger, Navarro's T uses four Stromberg 48 carbs to feed methanol to the destroked 179ci flathead Ford V8. Naturally, Navarro heads were used!

Right: Red paint with gold scallops set the race style for this '54 Ingels-Kraft roadster, aided by the chromed hairpins, complete with rear nerfs! A V8-60 flathead provides power.

Opposite: Barney Navarro produced speed equipment, including intakes and heads, proving their worth at the dry lakes. This '27T, his own car, recorded a 147mph top speed at El Mirage.

Classic Profile: **PIERSON BROS COUPE**

Bob and Dick Pierson took the rule book and stretched it to build their '34 coupe in 1950. The rules stated a minimum windshield height but not whether it was a vertical measurement, so the boys laid their windshield back to allow for a radical roof chop and hence minimal frontal area to reduce drag.

Campaigned as a lakes racer with various owners and engines until as recently as the early '90s, the car has been restored to its original configuration to rightfully take its place as a historically significant race car, complete with a fresh, Edelbrock-equipped Ford V8.

2D's trademark mailslot side windows hamper vision somewhat, but you only need to see in front of you when lakes racing! As many of the original parts as possible were used in the restoration, even down to the tie rod ends on the hairpins!

Right: Inside the Pierson coupe everything's there for a purpose, from the cut down wheel atop a '39 column, to the fuel tank next to the driver's sectioned B-25 bomber radar seat. The belly pan runs under the chassis and rear axle, encasing the running gear, but with a vent at the rear to release trapped air.

Below: Bruce Meyer tackles the hillclimb at the Goodwood Festival of Speed in 2000 in England—the mailslot windows of the Pierson coupe obviously making things "interesting" for the driver!

Right: Howdy Ledbetter's clone stood in for the original Ala Kart at the 50th Grand National Roadster Show, as the mainly Barris-built truck was undergoing restoration. AMBR winner in both '58 and '59, the detailed and chromed chassis featured coil springs at each corner, with airbags. The scallops are painted in a matching pattern on the undersides of the fenders.

Above: Although not an original '50s hot rod, Sweden's Tommy Classen shows what can be done with an original steel '32 roadster body and authentic early hot rod parts. From the Halibrand rear, and Firestone tires to the dropped original front axle, and the dressed 59AB flathead, this Deuce was good enough to take the Bruce Meyer Award for the best nostalgia rod at Oakland in 1998.

Classic Profile: TOMMY IVO'S T

TV and movie actor TV Tommy Ivo built his T after seeing Norm Grabowski's version, both becoming virtual blueprints for thousands of T buckets built during the next two decades. He also took his T to the dragstrip, where the race-prepared Nailhead Buick V8 he'd pulled from his full size race car netted him many 11 second timeslips, as well as the California Street Roadster Championship. With the roof and windshield removed, and a rollcage bolted in, the Ivo T was a fearsome track tool. Both Ivo and the T went on to appear in the movies, Ivo combining his career with racing all kinds of dragsters.

Right: The body for the T was found in the desert, the front half of a '25T phaeton to which Ivo added a drastically shortened Model A pick-up bed. Copying sprint car ideas, Ivo made a front four-link from Ford steering links, years before such items became common hot rod practice.

Below: The Model A chassis for the T was Z'd for less rake than Grabowski's version. Von Dutch stripped the T, which was sold in the late 1950s and gradually evolved into a show rod before Jack Rosen restored it as you see here. Widened and reversed steel wheels with whitewalls completed the look.

Right: The 402ci Buick Nailhead was pulled from Ivo's race car at the time, and over the years was injected, or ran two four barrels or six Strombergs in a quest for faster times. The car now wears Hilborn injection. A '37 LaSalle trans was hooked up to the Buick.

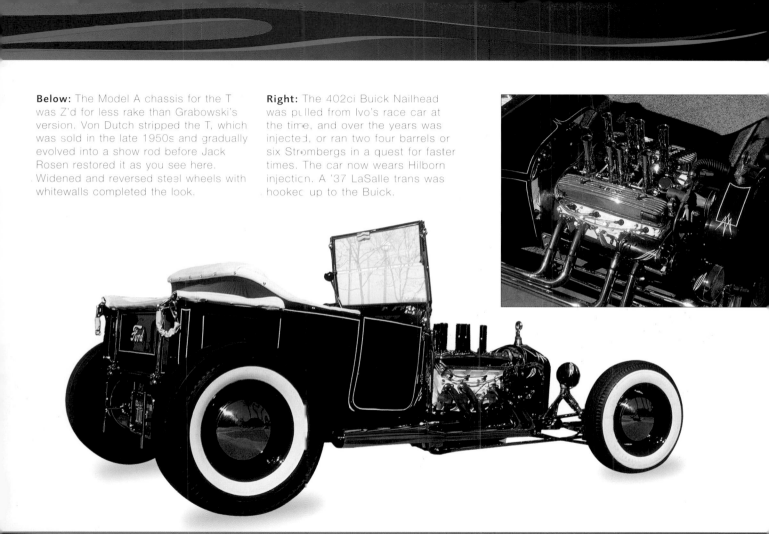

Opposite: This late '50s-built T bucket could certainly win any carb overkill awards, with eight carbs feeding its small block Chevy. With a drilled chromed axle and wide whites on chrome reversed rims, it looks like a model kit come to life.

Right: Originally built in '58 and stored in a garage for decades, this chopped and channeled '30/'31 Model A coupe wears its battle scarred green lacquer with pride.

Left: Larry Hook's Norm Wallace-built Detroit Autorama veteran is one of the finest original '50s show and go rods on the East Coast, and has been exhibited at Pebble Beach as well as LA's Petersen Museum. The Thickstun air cleaner sits atop twin 97s, themselves bolted to a SCoT supercharged flathead.

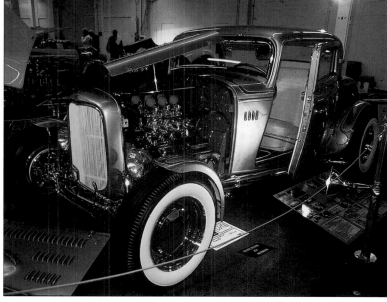

Left: Gary Peterson was 16 in '58 when he screwed together this full fendered Deuce coupe using a '51 331ci Chrysler hemi and Lincoln Zephyr trans. Untouched since, including dings, it would be a crime to paint this blue and white beauty.

Right: A six carbed '51 Chrysler 331ci hemi feeds power through a '46 LaSalle trans in this '32 three window. Gary Dusteson put the rod together in 1954. It placed First in Class at Oakland in 1959, then wound up on a used car lot a mere two years later.

Opposite: An Ardun overhead valve conversion, complete with blower graces the flathead V8 in this restored '50s-built '32 three window coupe. Another in Bruce Meyer's collection, and restored by So Cal Speed Shop, this one sees regular street use.

Classic Profile: *NORM GRABOWSKI'S T*

Anyone who remembers watching *77 Sunset Strip* will remember Norm Grabowski's T bucket, Edd "Kookie" Burns' Kookie Car. Norm can be regarded as the father of the T bucket, as he created a new style of T with his roadster in 1955. The car's rake came from its non-Z'd Model A frame and high A rear spring, while the near vertical '38 Chevy steering column was a new idea too.

Adding to the rod's unique look was the radically shortened Model A pick-up bed, and the '22 Dodge windshield, which was laid back on the cowl. It was one of a kind when it debuted, rather like its owner!

Right: The "suicide" front spring came about when Norm used modified '40 Ford wishbones and mounted the ends of them backwards on the '37 Ford tube axle, placing the spring behind the axle, and at the same time pushing the wheelbase forwards.

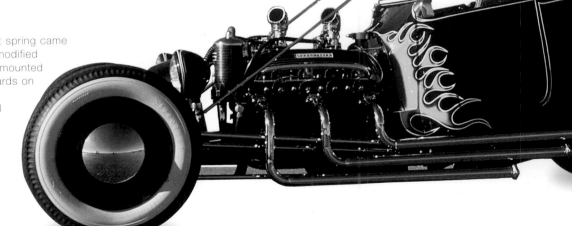

Right: Realizing that Ford's flathead V8 was probably about to lose its title as *the* hot rod engine of choice, Norm opted for a '52 Cadillac V8, increased in capacity to 354ci. Four Strombergs, and later a blower, boosted performance, along with a Winfield cam.

3

1960s

The 1960s were lean years for hot rodding. The introduction of drag strips in the '50s—places for hot rodders to race without endangering lives on public roads—took many rods away from the streets in the quest for more speed, while the dawn of the muscle car era later in the decade made building one's own car somewhat redundant. Others entered the show car arena, which became increasingly bizarre as the decade wore on. Social circumstances changed greatly in the '60s, and owning a hot rod just wasn't cool any more for many youngsters. Some persevered, however, until the retro rod boom of the 70s made the hobby popular once again.

Left: Sven Sandberg's Glowing Coupe debuted at Sweden's Hot Rod Show in '65. After a dubious career as a show car then a drag racer, Sven bought the coupe back in the mid '90s and restored it

Left: Not all rods are roadsters, sedans, and coupes, as this '32-'34 Ford pick-up attests. Nerf bars and skinny white bands on chrome reversed rims put this truck in the late 1960s, even if the stance is a little too low.

Opposite: This full fendered '30/'31 A roadster has, unusually, been heavily channeled, accounting for the strange occurrence where the front fender crosses the lower cowl.

Right: Rich Guasco is the only person to win back to back at Oakland, as this '29A on Deuce rails won AMBR in '61, followed in '62 by Guasco's Pure Hell AA/Fuel Altered winning the race car part of the trophy, since discontinued. The A was restored for the 50th anniversary show, though not strictly to its original form, as can be seen, with radial tires and a modern interior.

Right: Though Andy Kassa's '32 started its show career in the mid-'50s, the final version seen here only made a brief showing, just twice in 1964. George Barris fabricated the aluminum grille with single headlight, earning the car the name 'Cyclops.' Chopped and channeled, the three window also received a Z'd chassis to get it extra low, while everything that could be was chromed, including most of the parts on the '48 Mercury V8, right down to the water pumps.

Opposite: Dean Jeffries' Mantaray featured a one-off, one piece, assymetrical body constructed from 86 hand-formed sheets of aluminum over a steel framework. This was attached to a Masarati Formula One chassis, with an offset Ford Cobra 289ci motor and hand-blown bubble top.

Opposite: Tony LaMasa's version of an American sports car was this channeled '32 roadster powered by a stock '56 Corvette engine. The pinstriped and louvered rod also appeared on TV on the *Ozzie and Harriet Show*.

Below: Channeled to the max, this 1950s-era '31 roadster has been brought into the 1960s with the addition of five-spoke tires which have been fully chromed, along with lakes-style headers.

Classic Profile: **ED ROTH'S OUTLAW**

No account of hot rodding would be complete without at least once visiting the wild world of Ed "Big Daddy" Roth. Already painting cars and T-shirts for a living, the Outlaw was Roth's first foray into the messy world of fiberglass—the resin and mat laid over a plaster buck, with a Model A chassis, and Caddy engine for a base. With no-one to turn to for advice on the new product, Roth kept going until he got it right. He had to sell his A sedan to pay for the chrome, and there was a lot of it, from suspension parts to the individual headers, and even the oil pan.

The rest is history, with the Outlaw becoming one of the most successful show cars of the early '60s, touring the country behind any number of hearses Roth used as tow vehicles. Revell made a model of it, giving Roth his "Big Daddy" moniker at the same time, by which time he had moved on to build the Beatnik Bandit, Rotar, and the twin engined Mysterion.

Four carbs fed the Caddy motor, while the latest skinny dragster wire wheels were used on the front, straight or to the spindles with no brakes. The Outlaw followed the T bucket-build style, but with a totally hand-formed body and grille shell, incorporating quad headlights.

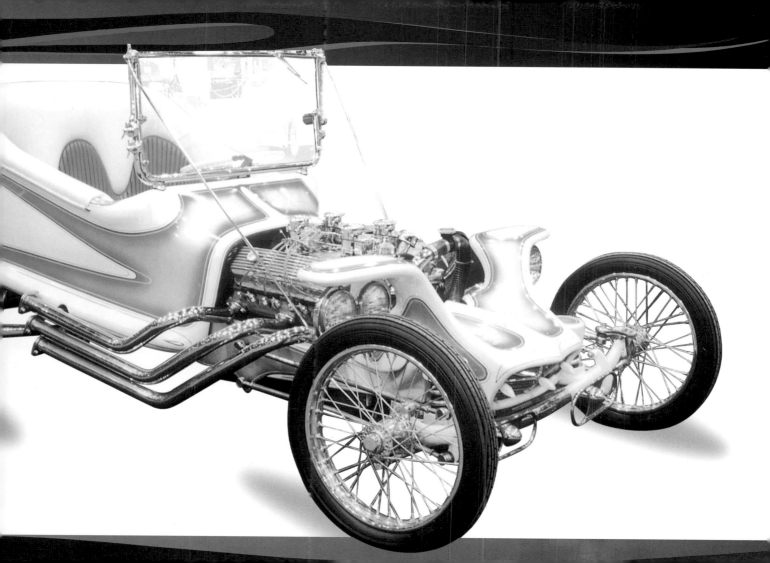

Opposite: George Barris is known for building customs, but when he took a shot at the AMBR competition in '62 with the Twister T he left with the trophy. Quad headlights, a custom grille insert, and green metalflake helped the '27 on '32 rails win.

Below: Ken Fuhrman's A on B rails was built in the '50s, and was the first to use fully chromed frame rails. This version, with plexiglass hood to display the Elco twin plug head-equipped flathead and a set of the first Torq Thrust magnesium American Racing wheels given to Fuhrman by ARE's owner, dates from '63.

Above: *Hot Rod* magazine's cover car in September '62, Don Waite's Model A roadster featured a destroked '52 De Soto motor displacing 252ci, and ran a best quarter mile time of 10.5 secs at 140mph. Purely a competition machine, the engine sat way back under the stock cowl.

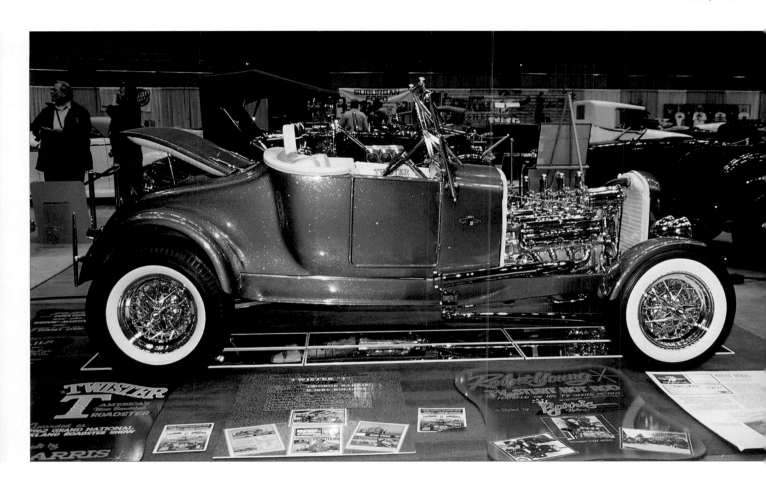

Right: Now part of Blackie Gejeian's collection of rods, the Emporer won the AMBR trophy in 1960. Built by Barris and owner Kirk Krikorian it features a fully chromed chassis, pearl white upholstery and six carbs atop a pair of Cragar inlet manifolds on the Caddy motor, as well as filled rear wheel wells and a one-off nose. Unrestored, including the upholstery and candy paint, the modern tires jar with the vintage feel.

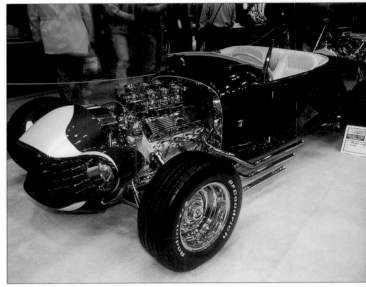

Left: A refugee from the gasser wars that prevailed on the drag strips during the late 1960s and beyond, this '41 Willys coupe now spends its time on the street and at shows. Fenderwell headers are now capped and feed into a full exhaust system. Modern rubber is used for safety should the coupe stray onto a race track at any time.

Right: The Centerline wheels and alternator are later additions but this '28/'29 lowboy—a channeled fenderless rod—is an average '60s hot rod. Bet the twin carbed small-block Ford provided plenty of fun, though!

Below: Mickey Himsl's Moonshiner 26T was shown at Oakland in 1963 in gold and purple metalflake with exhausts running up each side of the body and 12 spoke spindle mount front wheels. Himsl restored it to its previous guise with tiny 12in front wheels.

Left: Bo Jones' T Modified used the front half of a '26/'27T, narrowed to emulate the early track roadsters. Quarter elliptical springs suspended the I beam front axle, with lengthened split wishbones locating it. Hairpin radius rods did the same job at the rear. Jones' Modified is probably the most famous of its type.

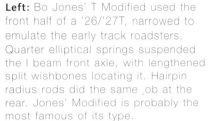

Right: If you didn't have the Red Baron as a model kit as a kid, you probably had the Hot Wheels version. This straight six-motored show car was loosely based on the T bucket concept, with a huge German helmet for a roof, machine guns on the cowl, and iron crosses everywhere.

Left: This 1937 Chevy coupe emulated the gassers that terrorized dragstrips across America during the '60s. The front sections of the hood and hood sides have been left intact, making for a strange looking abbreviated engine bay.

Below: Chuck Miller's Fire Truck won the Ridder Award in 1968. Plenty of imagination saw engine number 13 with a shorty ladder mounted to the side, a single seat behind an oval windshield, and blown Ford motivation. The running gear was a chrome shop owner's dream, though the 12 spoke front and Torq Thrust rear wheels were left in rough cast finish. Candy red covered the C cab body.

Left: Bob Reisner's hand-formed aluminum Invader featured two Pontiac engines feeding a rear end formed from parts of two Jaguar independent rears. Despite its wild show car appearance, Reisner actually drove it on the street, made the cover of *Hot Rod* magazine in '67 and won AMBR in that and the following year.

Right: High riding '32 five window exemplifies the appearance of '60s hot rods, with its nose-up stance, and white upholstery. Tunnel rammed big block Chevy flanked by zoomie headers is reflected in a polished aluminum firewall.

Opposite: Hand-formed from aluminum by Joe Wilhelm, Wild Dream took the AMBR trophy in '68, though it was painted lavender and wore a modified '32 grille at the time. The finned objects displayed by the car were the wheel centers from the original incarnation

Classic Profile: MOONEYHAM & SHARP '34

The number of hot rods on the streets in the '60s may have lessened, but the dragstrip still had its fair share—in fact, many race cars had been street driven until the advent of local drag strips took them beyond the realms of streetability. One of the most famous was the Mooneyham and Sharp "554" '34 coupe of Gene Mooneyham and Al Sharp. Mooneyham had raced the car, painted silver, as an A/Fuel coupe with Carl Johnson in the late '50s, but it wasn't until the partnership with Sharp, and a change from a 430ci Chrysler to a blown 390ci Chrysler, that the car appeared as it is remembered today, when it hit 152mph in 1960. Breaking the 150mph mark ensured the team received lots of publicity, making the car the most famous of its era, before the gassers appeared. Over the following three years times fell to 8.98 and the terminal speed rose to a best of 170.8, but by '64 Mooneyham had sold the coupe on and moved up to Fuel Dragster racing. The coupe today resides in Don Garlits' Museum of Drag Racing when it isn't running at nostalgia drag racing events. The "554" coupe was the forerunner of the Fuel Altered class and was responsible for generating much interest in such race cars.

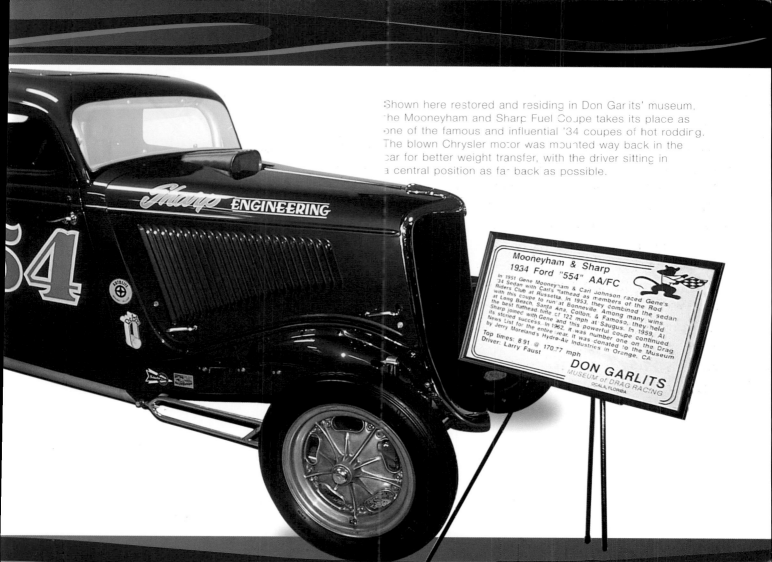

Shown here restored and residing in Don Garlits' museum, the Mooneyham and Sharp Fuel Coupe takes its place as one of the famous and influential '34 coupes of hot rodding. The blown Chrysler motor was mounted way back in the car for better weight transfer, with the driver sitting in a central position as far back as possible.

Mooneyham & Sharp
1934 Ford "554" AA/FC

In 1951 Gene Mooneyham & Carl Johnson raced Gene's '34 Sedan with Carl's flathead as members of the Rod Riders Club at Russetta. In '53, they combined the sedan with this coupe to run at Bonneville. Among many wins at Long Beach, Santa Ana, Colton, & Famoso, they held the best flathead time of 122 mph at Saugus. In 1959, Al Sharp joined with Gene and this powerful coupe continued its storied success. In 1962, it was number one on the Drag News List for the entire year. It was donated to the Museum by Jerry Moreland's Hydro-Air Industries in Orange, CA.

Top times: 8.91 @ 170.77 mph
Driver: Larry Faust

DON GARLITS
MUSEUM of DRAG RACING
OCALA, FLORIDA

4

1970s

The '70s has often been described as the decade that taste forgot, and looking back at some of the cars that emerged during those years, those commentators could have had a point! However, the paint schemes and modifications were neat at the time, and today all make up part of hot rodding's heritage.

Let's not forget, too, that the '70s saw the emergence of rod runs as we know it, the first Street Rod Nationals and Antique Drags. A new name emerged as well, "street rodding," in an effort to get away from the rebellious image hot rodding had previously been associated with.

Left: Four seater tubs, or phaetons, were rarer than T buckets, especially with fenders. Wire wheels, cowl lamps, mirrors and a motometer on the rad were all necessary parts in the 1970s, as were pleated or buttoned upholstery and a repro T steering wheel. A small-block Ford powers this tub.

Above: Show cars became more and more outrageous throughout the late 1960s and early 1970s, with Carl Casper's Popcorn Wagon shown here raising the ante when it appeared at the 1970 Detroit Autorama. Twin blowers and a high stance aided by the straight tube axle helped it achieve lasting fame when it was manufactured as an MPC model kit.

Left: Though panel painted and wearing slot mag wheels, the nose-high stance of this Chevy coupe indicate a '60s-built rod. Who knows, it was probably an old gasser race car put on the street

Below: Slot mag wheels, outside headers, and crazy paint locate this '28/'29 Model A coupe in the '70s, though the nerfs, channeled stance, and top chop point to it having been built sometime earlier.

Left: Think of '70s rods and the perennial T bucket probably comes to mind first, along with resto-rodded '32 roadsters. This example sports a tunnel ram-equipped small-block Chevy, ribbon paint, and no front brakes for the 12 spoke wheels. Long chrome four bars locate the axles, the front suicide style way out in front of the chromed T rad shell.

Opposite: The '70s saw a mild resurgence in popularity for customs, as this '39 ragtop shows. Though a bit high for a custom, the heavy chop and white roof fit the image, with the wide whites and 'capped steels.

Classic Profile: THE GRAFFITI COUPE

Is this the most famous hot rod coupe of them all? Automotive star of the movie *American Graffiti*, character John Milner's '32 coupe was bought by the production team as a rough but running hot rod, and spruced up and painted for its movie role. Much of the 1973 film's action happens in and around the five window, with the final scene pitting it successfully against a '55 Chevy in a dawn street race. The car is currently owned by Rick Figari, who had lusted after it since seeing the movie as an eight year old!

Right: The coupe is by no means perfect, but has been left as it was in the movie, even down to the camera-mounting holes in the chassis. It was meant to appear slightly rough on camera, typifying the kind of car a teenager might drive.

Above: The front license plate is the car's movie tag, the rear is its current one. The '57 Chevy rear axle is crudely mounted in chassis and is the view most contenders were supposed to see when they challenged the "fastest car in the valley."

Right: Rare Man-A-Fre intake was added for the movie, with four Rochester two barrel carbs. The engine is a mid-'60s 327 small-block Chevy with high performance heads. The short radiator and grille shell is a characteristic of the "Graffiti coupe."

Opposite: This '39 Mercury custom features moulded fenders and modified running boards with frenched headlights, and nerf bars. Red graphics incorporate flames, while the Merc's frameless door windows lend a different look to the chopped roof compared to a Ford of the same year. The rear side window has been eliminated during the chopping process, and Appleton spotlights added to bring a nostalgic touch to the custom.

Right: Guitarist Jeff Beck bought this Model B sedan called Super Prune in the United States and shipped it home to England. Though hot rodding was alive and well overseas, early steel Fords were rare, and parts such as Halibrand quick changes, and spindle mount 12 spoke wheels were unheard of in the 1970s. Nowadays, of course, especially since the advent of the Internet, rare parts and vintage tin can be found across the globe.

Below: Dubbed Boston Strangler, this fiberglass '23T roadster pick-up ran a 302ci small-block Chevy and dropped '32 axle with '40 Ford brakes. Halibrand wheels wrapped in L50 tires were covered by chromed fenders at the rear, while a Corvair provided the steering box.

Left: Night time cruising in a Model A coupe. Unchopped but sectioned, this '30/'31 has moulded rear fenders and a custom grille shell with quad headlights. Interestingly, it seems to have the same size tires at each corner.

Above: Typical English early '70s T bucket was done slightly differently to its US cousins. Strict laws meant fenders were required at each corner, while a steering rack was used in conjunction with an early Ford I beam axle. Power came from a Jaguar straight six.

Classic Profile: THE SUPER BELL COUPE

Jim Ewing of the Super Bell Axle Company built this radical '34 three window coupe and drove it all over America. Chopped and heavily channelled, the coupe would attract attention even without the track-style nose. Unfortunately, that grille caused cooling problems with such a small opening, but stepping down from a big block Chevy, to a small-block, and ultimately a V6 Buick motor, allowed Ewing to retain the distinctive nose. In a sea of '33 and '34 coupes, this is surely one anyone would remember.

Right: Naturally, as owner of Super Bell Axle Company at the time, Ewing's coupe ran one of his tube axles with the biggest drop available in order to bring the three window down out of the wind. Sometime after this picture was taken, the headlights were swapped for big, stock '34 lights. Disc brakes made sure the regularly driven coupe was safe.

Above: Sometimes Ewing ran the coupe with Firestone dirt track rear tires on Halibrand wheels, sometimes with Moon discs, and occasionally with Moon discs on the Halibrands! The Halibrand quick change can be seen under the modified rear pan, while the coupe's rake is noticeable in this shot.

Opposite: This unchopped '32 five window is heavily channeled but not sectioned as it first looks. The doors have been shortened and the lower body extended out to cover the exhausts. The radiator has been moved forward of the crossmember to accommodate the Ford V8.

Below: Resto-rodded Deuce five window featuring cowl lamps, wire wheels, bumpers, door handles, and subdued black paintwork with red accents.

Above: Take one stock '32 five window, lose the hood, bolt on a set of slot mags, and throw on some primer for instant cool. Don't forget the chrome air cleaner, too! The same would still work today, though a set of '40 Ford steels would probably replace the mags.

Opposite: This wire wheeled and wind wing be-decked resto-rod roadster was obviously providing plenty of fun for its occupants, including those in the rumble seat. Seeing rods parked so often at shows and cruises, it's easy to forget their main purpose—that is, for driving. Out on the road is where these cars give the most pleasure.

Above: Lonnie Gilbertson's T won the AMBR in '71 while in a candy red and running Webers, and then again in '75 in this guise with independent suspension and a blower. Fad Ts are rarely seen full fendered.

Right: Just out cruising in a flamed T bucket. Skinny brakeless wire wheels and a tunnel rammed small-block in a lightweight car will make for interesting moments.

Below: This channeled Model A roadster was most likely built a while before this picture was taken, if those widened rear wheels and the flathead V8 are anything to go by.

Right: Diminutive English Austin Ruby that was fully street legal but regularly drag raced by builder Pip Biddlecombe in the '70s. Power comes from a Daimler "baby" hemi V8.

Above: Pete Hurrell gave his '35 Hillman the full resto-rod treatment in 1978, even retaining the stock I beam front axle. Out back, a Jaguar independent rear suspension was fed by a Ford V6 motor.

Classic Profile: *NOSTALGIA T*

Nostalgia's nothing new—Dan Holck was at it back in the '70s! Taking three and a half years to screw together this T, he opted for a by now out of date Ford flathead V8, early Ford running gear, and chromed reverse rims with narrow white band tires. A Halibrand quickie was hung on a Model A spring with shock absorbers from a tractor seat, while an original drop-forged '32 axle was mounted in front of the brass radiator. The Iowa resident even made his own fibreglass T body and sprayed the red acrylic. Truly an owner-built roadster from start to finish.

Right: With parts collected from an eclectic mix of sources, such as Corvair steering, tractor seat shocks, and early Ford running gear, Dan Holck tackled the whole build himself, apart from the upholstery in his roadster, even making his own body, steering wheel, and seats.

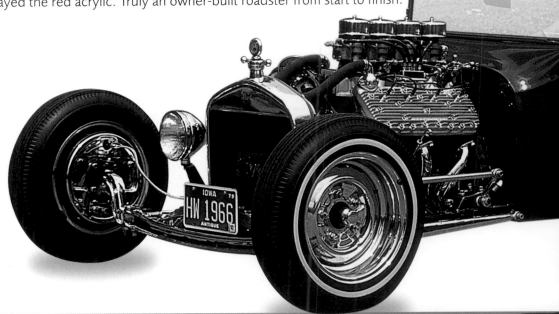

Right: The 258ci flathead was bored ⅛in and filled with an Isky cam and Jahns pistons, with Offenhauser heads and a quartet of Ford 94 carbs on the outside. Homemade exhausts take care of spent gases, while a W&H Du-Coil provides sparks to the 6v system. A Weber flywheel links the motor to a '39 Ford tranny.

Left: After the virtual disappearance of hot rods from the streets in the '60s, the '70s saw a resurgence in the popularity of T buckets, possibly since they were relatively cheap and quick to build. It took a while for front brakes to catch on though!

Opposite left: The two way flip front on this Chevy sedan must have made panel alignment a chore! Flames and panel graphics make for busy paintwork, while all the stock trim has been retained and the light cowlings dipped in the chrome vat.

Right: The "broken back" look of a T usually came about as the engine was almost always horizontal to line up with the rear axle, while the body was mounted at an angle in order to clear the axle and allow some interior room.

Opposite: Chopped in the '50s and then left to decay until Roger Mellman resurrected it, this '39 Ford coupe was treated to a "built" Oldsmobile 425ci V8 with triple carbs, TH400 trans, and '57 Chevy rear end. A Mor-Drop front axle was used to bring the front end down. while '49 Plymouth bumpers and lights all round from a '40 Ford improve its appearance.

Below: When most hot rods still used beam axles, Brian Lucas' '32 roadster featured homebrewed independent front suspension to complement the Jaguar IRS. The bobbed-fendered rod was finished in candy red, though strangely the doors were never cut from the one-piece fiberglass body to enable easier access.

Above: Fully fendered and sporting a hood, this "almost a C-cab" pick-up just needs a couple of stray dogs in the bed with that signwriting!

Left: With the roof in place a T roadster could appear really tall! Blown motor must have been mucho fun in this little tub.

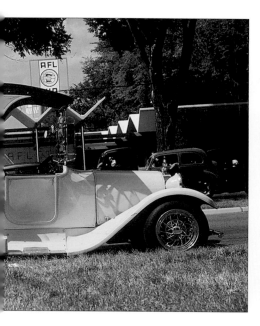

Right: Named "Yesterday's Dreams" this T roadster was Brian Bates' version of a fully fendered T. With a Daimler hemi V8 and Jag IRS, the rod featured many homemade brass items, such as the headlights and grille shell.

Opposite: A nicely detailed '28/'29 Model A roadster pick-up sits just right over orange wires, the choice of tires giving a slight "rubber rake." The owner opted to add a later '30/'31A stainless grille shell, probably to give the front end some sparkle.

Below: Model T coupes are pretty rare as rodder fodder, and can look a bit strange, though this suicide front suspended example pulls it off with a triple carbed small-block and big 'n' little rubber. Why such a tall roof? So originally the driver could wear his hat while driving.

Opposite: Shortened pick-up bed on this early Model A truck gives the finished rod a stumpy appearance, accentuated by those exhausts. To make room in the engine bay for the somewhat larger than stock motor, the radiator was moved forward.

Below: "Speed Freak" was a blown V6 powered high-riding Fordson, or Thames delivery, running mis-matched Fenton and American Racing "daisy" mags. The tiny size dictated the driver sat behind the B pillar.

Above: With moulded rear fenders, this flamed and channeled '32 coupe enjoys a spot of cruising. Lakes style exhausts were seemingly on everything in the 1970s. A grille mounted in front of crossmember makes the car appear much longer.

Above: A '40 Mercury custom has had the headlights frenched and fender skirts added, with only the whitewall now visible beneath them. The chopped carson-style top was very popular when these cars were big news the first time round.

Opposite left: This barely street legal Model B roadster was mainly used for drag racing, though here the driver has a little fun lighting up the tires at a rod run.

Left: Chevy sedan delivery, very understated in gunmetal grey metallic with chrome wire wheels. Most deliveries in this decade were signwritten, but this owner exercised restraint and it looks better for it. A slight nose down stance lets bystanders know this is no nicely restored stocker.

Classic Profile: THE CALIFORNIA KID

For car buffs the star of the made for TV movie, *The California Kid*, was Pete Chapouris' black and flamed '34 coupe, but this was no TV prop, as it was Chapouris' own hot rod. Its appearance on the cover of *Rod & Custom* magazine in 1973 brought it to the attention of the film's producer, who hired it for the movie, swapping the Halibrand wheels it usually wore for red steels and hubcaps. *The California Kid* script on the doors was added for the film, and has stayed to this day as the name became synonymous with the coupe.

Right: Chapouris bought the coupe as a battered ex-hot rod, with the roof chop already done and filled, and swapped over the running gear from his previous rod, a T. It was while building the coupe that he met Jim "Jake" Jacobs, subsequently forming the partnership that became Pete & Jake's Hot Rod Parts.

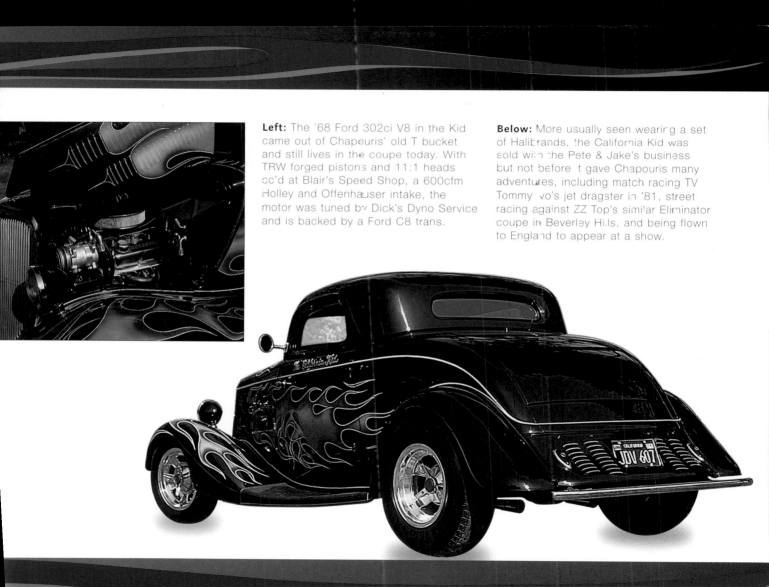

Left: The '68 Ford 302ci V8 in the Kid came out of Chapouris' old T bucket and still lives in the coupe today. With TRW forged pistons and 11:1 heads cc'd at Blair's Speed Shop, a 600cfm Holley and Offenhauser intake, the motor was tuned by Dick's Dyno Service and is backed by a Ford C8 trans.

Below: More usually seen wearing a set of Halibrands, the California Kid was sold with the Pete & Jake's business but not before t gave Chapouris many adventures, including match racing TV Tommy vo's jet dragster in '81, street racing against ZZ Top's similar Eliminator coupe in Beverley Hills, and being flown to England to appear at a show.

Left: Roof chopped vans are rare sights as they involve lots of bodywork, but this Austin Devon van originally started life as a Countryman, a sort of station wagon with side windows. Once the aluminum body was chopped and those windows paneled in, Triumph TR3 roadster rear fenders were added and brick red candy over silver paint covered the sheetmetal. A little Ford four banger powered the everyday driver.

Opposite: Most British cars are too small to swallow a V8 motor without major modification, but the long hood of this Hillman four door easily covered a 327ci Chevy motor. Apart from the Pos-a-traction tires on domestically produced slot mags, the resto-rod appearance even included a rear luggage rack. Two tone paint furthered the resto image.

Left: Early Fords tend to be the basis for most hot rods but there are plenty who are drawn to other marques, such as the Mulliner-bodied 1930 Daimler DB19 here. Admittedly very obscure, but there's little chance of finding yourself parked next to another one at a rod run! The 3in chopped sedan wears Appliance Fine Wire wheels and runs under the name of Al Ca'blown, referring to the supercharged Buick V8.

Opposite: Ford Anglias, or Populars as they are called in England, have long been associated with hot rodding, and were sought after for use as gassers in the '60s. This Popular, however, used to be a race car of a very different kind, as it was once a circuit racer, starting its career in '67. Berpop, as it's known, is powered by a fuel injected bored Buick V8 with adjustable independent suspension all round, based on Jaguar components. A space frame chassis and dual circuit brakes were surely unique when this car was first put on the road.

Classic Profile: THE HENWAY

"What's the make of that truck?" "A Henway."

"What's a Henway?" "About three pounds!"

And that was the origin of the name of Norm Grabowski's hand-built truck, the Henway. As well as a neat car builder, Grabowski is a dab hand at woodcarving—his cartoonish shifter knobs are highly prized among the hot rod fraternity. So it should be no surprise that he undertook all the woodwork on the Henway himself, and it was in the flatbed truck that he relocated from southern California to Arkansas.

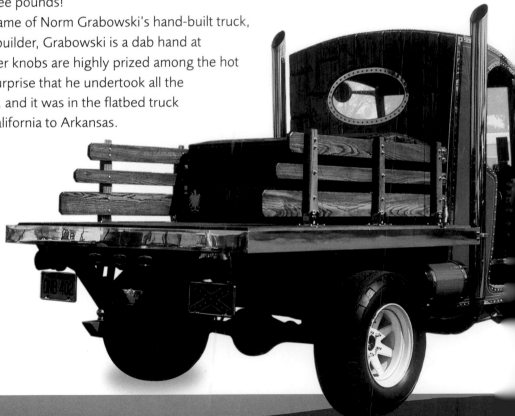

Right: The hand-built wood and sheetmetal C cab-style truck featured chrome exhaust stacks at the rear of the cab with removable staked bed sides, and a lockable trunk on the flatbed. The towbar was necessary as Grabowski used this truck as a truck!

Left: Kooky frontal appearance was part of the Henway's charm, and a Grabowski trait. There have even been replicas built, though the original is tucked away in Grabowski's garage in Arkansas. Disc brakes were an usual safety addition on rods in the '70s, but necessary on a high mileage driver.

Above: Show cars had become totally separated from what the average rodder was building for the street in the '70s, as Jack Keefe's Stage Fright coach shows. Though these aren't the original tires, the rest of the over-the-top show car remains as it was when originally built.

Right: Black and flames has become a very traditional hot rod colour scheme, this '32 Ford hiboy proving that such a combo always looks cool. With large stock headlights, chromed wires, and hairpin radius rods, it's a look that was hard to beat.

Below: Sidepipes and chrome five spokes shout mid-1970s on this '39 coupe, as does high stance. Fat tires at all four corners were popular, too. Stock trim and bumpers remained on this rod even after its repaint in blue with blue flames.

Left: Fad style build was unusual for '26/'27T body style, though this pick-up looks like lots of fun with its blown and injected motor in such a short wheelbase. Oh, and no front brakes either! A sectioned '32 grille gives the front end a different look.

Below: Digger style '23T bucket with zoomie headers took the T concept about as close to the dragstrip refugee look as was possible on the street. With big slicks and a blown Chrysler hemi, the wheelie bars were probably frequently in contact with the ground!

Opposite: This high-stepping '32 three window coupe was powered by a twin carbed and tunnel rammed Ford motor. With a stock height roof the full fendered rod retained the original bumpers but not the hood. Chromed Tru Spoke wires were wrapped in BF Goodrich T/A radials, a new type of tire in the 1970s which would offer rodders much more choice in terms of tire width, grip, and handling.

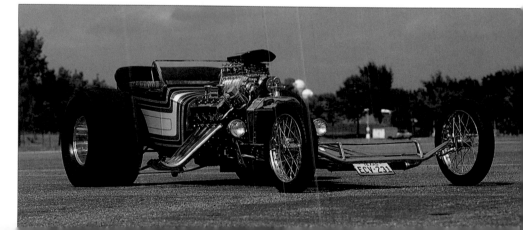

Left: A '28/ 29 Model A roadster body on a '32 chassis is one of the all time great hot rod combinations requiring slight pinching of the frame rails a the cowl.

Opposite left: A four carbed small block Chevy powered this very low T bucket, using a glass high back 1915 bodyshell A chromed Jag rear and tube front were offset by brass rad and lights.

Below: Whether this chopped Anglia is an ex-dragstrip warrior or a fresh street rod isn't recorded, but those 12 spokes, wheelie bars, and scoop poking through the hood point towards the former.

Classic Profile: '32 HIBOY ROADSTER

The 1932 Ford roadster has come to be regarded as the quintessential hot rod or street rod. With its fenders and running boards removed, even the exposed chassis is a thing of beauty, with its swage line running front to rear, and tapering upwards at the cowl. This roadster, with its chrome wire wheels, flamed paint, and brown pleated seat is a great example of where street rodding was heading towards the end of the decade—the dropped tube front axle and telescopic shocks showing the way towards aftermarket components rather than refurbished early Ford parts.

Right: Though no resto rod by any means, the lines of this '32 were still interrupted by wind wings, mirrors, and stock door hinges, all things that would disappear in a few short years in the search for total smoothness.

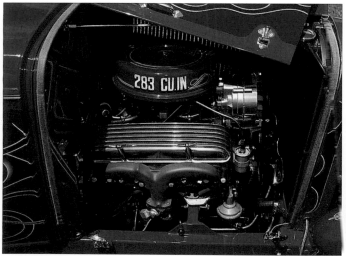

Above: No guessing what size this small block is, it's right there on the air cleaner! Alternator made wiring a street rod much simpler than the generators of old. A small-block Chevy fits so neatly in the engine bay of a '32, you'd think it was designed that way.

Right: Buttoned and pleated leather or Naugahyde was a popular choice for upholstery in the '70s, usually in brown too! Brown carpet and banjo-style steering wheel finish off this particular deuce cockpit.

Opposite: T buckets such as this provided plenty of opportunity for a showman to indulge himself. Fully chromed axle housings and suspension parts were commonplace, and monster tires on full width axles made Ts probably the widest and wildest cars on the streets. Here, we see the "big and little" ethos taken to extremes. Imagine the weight of that blown motor on those skinny cycle front tires.

Above: Very late in the decade split rim wheels such as these began to make an appearance, providing a look completely different to the mag wheels hitherto on the market.

Right: Phil Cool's blown 427 L88-powered Deuce roadster took the AMBR award in '78, after years of wacky show cars gave way to real hot rods again on the circuit. Traditional split wishbone suspension front and rear, and a perfect stock body marked the return to normality.

Above: Roof styles on T roadsters had changed, and with the ability for the occupants to sit in rather than on Ts, those roofs came down in height.

Left: Paul Wayling's much modified '39 Plymouth looks completely different after getting chopped and shortened, with scratchbuilt front fenders, and an altered '32 commercial grille shell.

Right: The bodywork on Pete Fowler's '30 Model A sedan delivery was almost totally stock, with straight yellow paint, though the tires sticking out the rear fenders and the blown small block let you know Dirty 30 could deliver the goods.

Opposite: The end of the decade saw more people tackling long distance trips in their street rods, and a trailer was usually required, as even with a sedan delivery such as this example there was little room for luggage. This suicide front suspended '32 on home-brewed chassis was captured on film a long way from home at the NSRA Street Rod Nationals in St Paul, Minnesota.

Above: Ray Evans screwed together this neat extended wheelbase T bucket using a straight six Ford motor, creating a fabulous effect with six exhaust pipes running down the side of the car. Long four bars located the front end with equally long ladder bars at the rear. The T remains in the same show-worthy condition in Ray's home garage to this day.

5

1980s

The 1980s brought the biggest surge of interest to the hobby since just after World War II. It also brought many new trends, such as Fat Attack, graphics, the smooth look, the introduction of billet aluminum, nostalgia rods, lower ride heights, "dare to be different", and much more. It meant building a rod could be done in any one of many styles and a builder didn't have to tread the same path as his or her contemporaries. The booming aftermarket business helped in a huge way too, as the choice of new parts, particularly fiberglass reproduction bodies, repro chassis, and alloy wheels, had never been greater, opening the hobby to people who up until then had never dreamed they'd be able to build their own rod.

Left: The late '80s saw nostalgia gain ground. While this looks like a '34 coupe with fenders and hood removed, it's actually a fresh car with a glass body.

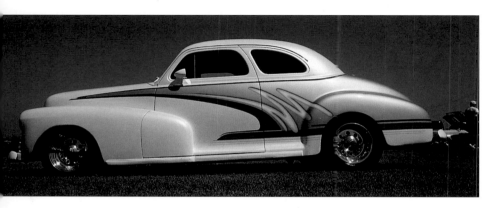

Left: White is an unusual color to see on street rods, though this Chevy coupe has graphics and faded paint added to break it up. This style of graphics was very popular for a while, but soon dated a car. The monochromatic look was starting to make inroads on the scene, as the painted bumpers and late model door mirrors here show.

Opposite: Graphics were de rigueur in the '80s with, seemingly, the more the better—and not always complementing the car's lines. This '36 Ford sedan wasn't strong on subtlety, and the stock accoutrements like bumpers and horn grilles were at odds with the graphics and color-coded windshield wiper.

Right: This '32 roadster has updated versions of the old scallop design seen on lakes racers for the previous two decades, flowing from hood side vents. Styles were a little mixed, as the hi-tech billet look was beginning to appear, but the resto-style bumpers, wind wings, and running boards could still be seen.

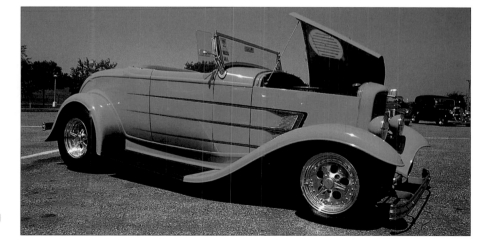

Classic Profile: *1937 CHEVROLET*

This '37 Chevy sedan is a typical example of late '70s/early '80s street rodding.
A sea of brown covers both the exterior and interior, while the choice of base car marked
the beginning of a trend in the move away from Ford-based rods, where models
previously considered ugly or not "cool" began to gain acceptance. Sedans also
began to make sense to rodders with families, as well as making long distance rod
running a more attractive proposition
than a roadster or cramped coupe.

Right: With seats and tilt steering
column lifted from a late model, this
Chevy must have been state of the art
for its time. Other up-to-the-minute
items include the ICE, CB, and air
conditioning. Chromed window
garnish moldings break up the mix
of brown mohair, vinyl, and cloth.

Left: Chrome wire wheels complement this Chevy, especially as it has extra chrome accessories, such as the front bumper guard and chrome fender welting, in addition to all the factory trim.

Above: This tall center door Model T sedan employs plenty of brass accessories and trim, complemented by gold striping on the body. Jaguar independent rear suspension has been liberated from its stock "cage", and is now fully visible, completely chromed, and detailed.

Left: This Chevrolet sedan has been updated, though still "keeps it in the family" with modern running gear from the same manufacturer, even down to the later model steel wheels with beauty rings.

Below: Model A highboy, a classic combination of a '28/'29 body on '32B chassis rails. Color coding became popular in the '80s, seen on the windshield frame and grille insert.

Left: Resto rods still had their place in the '80s, though the ride height had become to come down closer to what we see today. This fully loaded stock height Model A coupe even retains the stainless steel firewall trim, though interestingly has opted for smaller than stock diameter headlights

Opposite: Yellow '30/'31 Model A is an update on the American Graffiti '32 coupe, with its chopped roof, outside exhausts, multi-carb set-up, and sectioned Deuce grille shell, though the chromed five spokes, four bar, and wide low profile tires place it in a more modern timeframe.

Classic Profile: TRACK T MODIFIED

Quick, fun, and relatively inexpensive to build, circle track-inspired Modifieds started appearing at rod runs during the 1980s. Take the front half of a T Touring body, or any small two seat "bucket," and narrow it, modify a T or A frame or fabricate a simple new one, add a Model A rear spring and crossmember, and quarter elliptical-sprung I beam on split wishbones, and you've the basis of a fun hot rod. This example uses a Halibrand quick change center section in the early Ford rear axle and a long, upswept exhaust slash cut above the left hand rear tire.

Right: Big Model T headlights give a vintage feel to this Modified, aided by the Ford wire wheels, single rear light, and the four-spoke steering wheel. Using a Model A high arched rear spring enables it to be mounted above the axle without any clearance problems.

Left: With a narrowed body in such a short wheelbase, four bangers make ideal powerplants, though V6s have also been popular in such cars. They'll return respectable performance too in such a lightweight vehicle. Hidden under a hood, they don't have to be vintage appearing either, with a modern motor providing more reliability and power for trouble-free enjoyment.

Right: A small diameter wood-rimmed, four-spoke steering wheel tops the short column with early appearing gauges in a machine-turned dash. Pedal pads and dice shifter aren't quite so in keeping with the retro feel, but if the owner likes them, why not? The buttoned and pleated seat is comfortable in the cramped cockpit.

Right: With an explosion in the number of modern wheel designs available, most machined from solid billet, street rodders suddenly had a whole new look opened up to them. Combined with color coding throughout the vehicle, it was one of the most influential and important changes in direction the hobby seen.

Left: The Ford wires on this '28A have been widened to accept a pair of desirable Firestone dirt track tires, while the tri-power-equipped, small-block Chevy wears a set of headers with somewhat minimal ground clearance.

Right: With the huge street legal tires becoming available in the '80s from manufacturers such as Mickey Thompson, old favorites such as Ts could take on an even more cartoonish appearance. Though brass was still popular, and probably always will be on Ts, the addition of front brakes on most was an improvement from a safety viewpoint. The latter half of the decade would see beer barrel gas tanks fading from popular use.

Left: Nostalgia, '80s style! The family Jewel '41 Willys coupe harked back to the gasser wars of the '60s, though whether it's an ex-race car or just inspired by them, only the owner would know. Whichever, those Centerline wheels and Kelly tires don't date from the '60s.

Above: Another classic A on B rails, Simon Lane's '28A ran a supercharged Ford flathead with rare speed equipment. Those finned front brake drums are from a Buick, a popular conversion more for looks than improved heat dissipation on early Ford brakes.

Right: Change the wheels and tires on this '32 roadster, and it could almost be a stocker if it weren't so low. Fully fendered rods eliminate hassle in areas with strict fender laws.

Below: Equally as important as the billet smooth look was the retro movement which began to gain ground in the '80s, especially in England and Sweden. It would reach its peak worldwide some ten years later, but the mid '80s saw the debut of rods such as this period perfect baby blue Deuce three window, complete with heavy roof chop, whitewall crossply tires and early Ford running gear. Drilled front axle and split "bones" were about as traditional as one could get.

Classic Profile: '34 THREE WINDOW

Ford's 1934 coupe, or Model 40 to give it its correct title, has become something of an icon in the world of hot rodding. The archetypal rod may be a '32 Ford, but the '34 has formed the basis for many of the hobby's landmark and seminal cars. Though not a well known car, this '34 coupe should give some idea of why the design is so popular. From the distinctive curved grille to the unique rear pan, the design is arguably more graceful than the '32.

Right: The stepped firewall of the '33 and '34 Fords doesn't lend itself as well aesthetically as its predecessors to running hoodless, and in fact the welting round the cowl gives away that this car usually runs a hood. Nerf bars on the front replace the bumper while the roof has been chopped, further accentuating the car's already smooth flowing lines.

Right: GMC superchargers can be found on cranes, trucks, and other industrial machines and vehicles. They have also been found to work particularly well on V8 automotive engines, here on a small-block Chevy. Manifolds, drive systems, and carburetor adapters are all available for a wide variety of applications—adding a blower is one of the most significant additions one can make to a motor, visually and performance-wise.

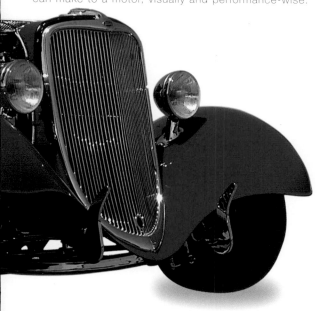

Right: The large fluted headlight lenses give this Model A pick-up its look, unique in that it features a rounded cab back rather than the usual flat design with quarter panels behind the doors. Louvres in the hood top allow hot air to escape from the engine bay.

Opposite: Richard Gardner was the proud builder of a '32, except instead of a Ford, his was a British Wolseley Hornet. With a custom-built Super Bell dropped tube front axle and a Jaguar IRS, the Candy red over silver four-door hood hid a Daimler hemi V8, while Richard rode in style on champagne Connolly leather.

Left: Ray Austin's little roadster was built from an English Model Y, which is very similar to a '34 in looks but scaled down to about three-quarter size. Only available in two or four-door sedan form, the roadster is entirely scratch-built from the B pillar back, with both the cowl and door tops modified from a closed car. Baby Moon hubcaps on steel wheels lend it a nostalgic look.

Above: Here's an oddball one—you'll really have to know your early autos to get it, or be a fan of the marque. It's a 1929 Nash coupe—rare enough in stock form, but even rarer rodded. Bodily stock, the yellow coupe runs Ford V6 running gear and chrome wire wheels with white lettered BF Goodrich rubber.

Left: Black and flamed track T based, unusually, on a '23 body with turtle deck. The narrow hood conceals a Ford Pinto OHC four cylinder motor—more than enough power for such a small light vehicle. Nerf bars and outside exhausts hark back to original circle track racers.

Below: C cab T delivery truck runs a T grille shell, dropped tube axle and modern headlights inside earlier headlight shells. Single four barrel carburetor on a tunnel ram provides the "tall engine" look yet retains some fuel economy.

Classic Profile: **ZZ TOP Eliminator '34**

If not as well known as the *American Graffiti* '32, then the Eliminator '34 coupe built for Texan band ZZ Top by Don Thelan's Buffalo Motor Cars, must surely come a close second. Band member Billy Gibbons' love for hot rods and customs led to the coupe being commissioned and subsequently appearing in three of the band's music videos—doing more to promote the hobby than anything since *American Graffiti*, and making a whole new generation aware of such cars' existence. A worldwide tour to promote the band's album saw the coupe displayed at record stores across the globe, as well as at concerts with the band.

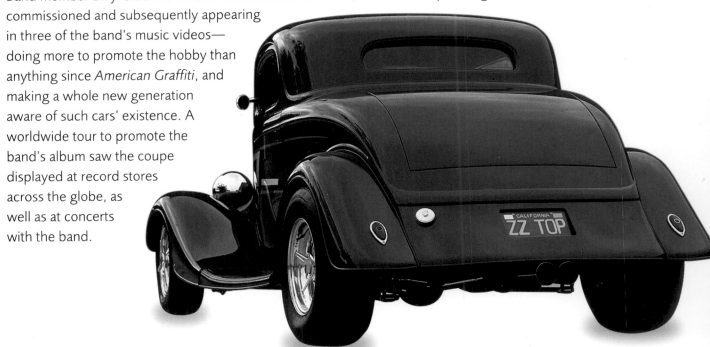

Opposite: If you weren't sure, that license plate says it's the original ZZ Top Eliminator coupe. These 1939 Ford teardrop rear lights replace the originals on the rear fenders, with that license frenched into the rear pan. As an ambassador for hot rodding, a bright red coupe is about as attention-grabbing as it gets. Apart from the split-rim alloy wheels, chromed windshield frame, and headlights, chromework on the coupe is conspicuous by its absence, though it predates the billet era, with rubber running board covers and exposed stockhinges.

Above: One of the most copied graphics for a while, the ZZ signature could be seen on hundreds of hot rods around the world in the mid '80s, usually on red coupes! The small-block Chevy-powered Eliminator is a rodder's favorite—Billy Gibbons even had another identical coupe built, as the original was away on tour so much. After the initial tour, the coupe went on the road with ZZ Top's later car, CadZZilla, and a pair of HogZZilla motorcycles. The second coupe was driven by Gibbons, and featured a fiberglass body where the original was steel.

Below: This gorgeous brandywine '40 Ford coupe has been chopped—no mean feat on a roof this curvaceous, and had the drip rails removed. The chrome five spokes fill the wheelwells perfectly, and wouldn't *you* leave the hood off if you had a six-carbed blown small block to show off?

Right: As well as the smooth billet look, the '80s also gave us Pro Street. Spawned from the Pro Stock drag racing class, it was more usually found on later full bodied cars, but this '32 Ford sports the trend's large rear tires inside stock bodywork, Supertrapp mufflers, and over-engined image.

Above: A rod for all occasions. Many rodders tend not to stop at just one car—this pair providing warm and cold weather cruising. It also shows just how small a Model A is.

Left: This heavily chopped Oldsmobile features almost the full arsenal of hot rodders' tricks—slanted pillars, tunneled lights, louvers front and rear, sliding sunroof, frenched license plate, molded front fenders, raised rear arches, and a channeled body.

Opposite: The owner of this early Model A wasn't content with just flaming the front end of his sedan, but opted to flame the roof too, making an eye-catching statement. The rest of the rod is fairly conservative, but the paint says all that needs to be said!

Below: A chopped and louvered Chevy two-door sedan with minimalist graphics displays the nose down in-the-weeds stance that became the norm during the '80s, getting away from the high riding look of the previous decade.

Opposite top: Compare the amount of room in the cockpit of this channelled '27T lowboy with the Model B below it, and you'll appreciate the relative comfort of the later model. That's not to say the '27 isn't an absolute blast to drive though, with wind in the hair and bugs in the teeth.

Right: Rod runs and cruises are social events just as much as they are for looking at the other cars in attendance. You'll pick up more ideas and tips by participating than can be gleaned from magazines, but be prepared to make friends!

Opposite bottom: With the sun glinting off the chrome, this is perfect roadster weather, one reason roadsters became so popular in southern California during hot rodding's infancy. Nothing says "hot rod" better than a red '32 hiboy.

Classic Profile: *1937 FORD SEDAN*

By the early to mid '80s street rods were getting smoother and lower. They were also becoming more refined too, and not just by having air conditioning or electric windows either, but because owners and builders started incorporating new car technology, with the latest advances in electronic management systems, suspension parts, engines, and accessories. Outward appearances were also changing, with fit and finish improving, and use of such items as bonded glass, late model door mirrors, handles, and third brake lights.

Right: Replacing the factory side vents in the hood, this '37 now has one large vent recessed into the panel. Unique two-tone paint scheme and detailed wheels help it stand out in a crowd.

Left: V-butted bonded glass replaces the '37s stock windshield and rubber, while the smoothed dash houses a simple gauge panel above the tilt steering column. A factory center console is extended up to the dash, while the use of factory vents, door pulls, and arm rests modernizes the Ford's pre-war design. The white interior and upholstery, and blue carpets integrate the exterior and interior, while the billet aluminum dash panel and black center of the console break up what would otherwise be a very monochromatic cabin.

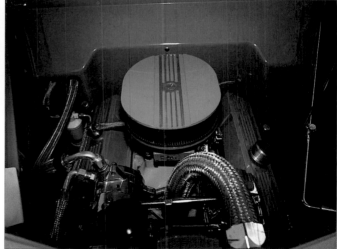

Right: The painted look continues to the underhood area, where the Chevy small block wears milled ally rocker covers and air cleaner, though they have been painted and detailed for a different appearance. Likewise, the carb and intake manifold have been painted body color. Braided hoses are used throughout for both safety and appearance, being much more pleasing on the eye than old rubber hoses. A recessed firewall provides the space required to fit the longer than stock motor.

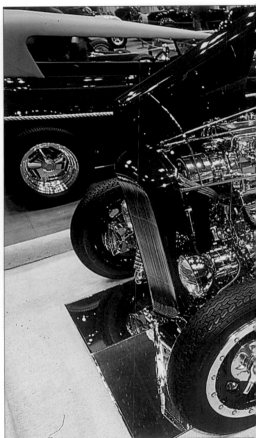

Below: With a four bar up front and a triangulated version of the same out back, this Deuce hiboy was as state of the art as they came back in the '80s, and sported a graphic that was popular on this body style at the time.

Right: Big John Siroonian took the AMBR trophy in '81 with this 6-71 blown Gurney Weslake Ford engined '32. Built by some of the hobby's top "names," the rod used an original body that had been a hot rod for most of its life.

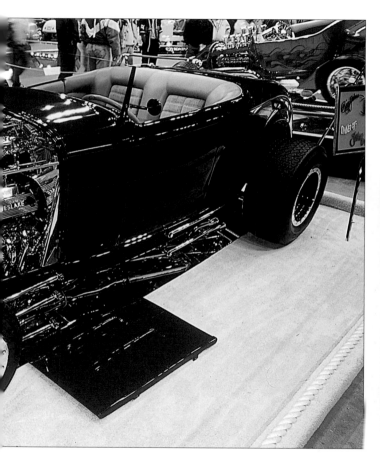

Below: Well known hot rodder Pete Chapouris put this fiberglass '27 together for his father, and though it used four bar suspension, aluminum windshield posts, and a billet dash, it retained a traditional hot rod image. Originally built with blackwall radials, it now runs whitewall crossply tires to enhance that look further

Opposite: This full, and widened, fendered '27T barely hides a big block Chevy under its hood. Trick independent front suspension is supported by American racing "daisy" mags. Unusual rod runs match wider rear wheels.

Below: Aftermarket painted wire wheels hide vented disc brakes on a dropped tube axle. Trim rings, hubcaps, and windshield frame are almost the only chrome accents on this completely color keyed car, yet it refrains from being "too red."

Opposite: Not only is this a classic '28 on '32 rails hiboy, it's the late Bill Burnham's roadster. Burnham's pull-no-punches column in *Street Rodder* magazine was a favorite for many. Ol' Blue, as the rod is called, features a 4in stretched frame to accommodate the 390ci big block Ford V8, and is seen here at Bonneville, a trip it made with Burnham at the wheel every year.

Above: Pick-up trucks have always been popular rodder fodder—this '32 Ford continues the tradition. Bobbed rear fenders give it a tough, abbreviated look from behind, a neat chromed nerf bar finishing off the rear end.

Right: Proving that a cool rod could be built on a budget, Gary Morgan put this T bucket together with Moon discs covering steel wheels and a Ford four banger motor hidden under the hood. The power bulge covers the carburetor.

Opposite: The Pro Street look hit street rodding big time in the '80s—Ian Dawes was one of the first with this '40 Willys coupe. Back then there weren't any fiberglass repro Willys' about, so if you saw one, you knew it was the real deal. Ian's ran a big-block Chevy to back up the tough image, though the "stranded at the roadside" look was purely for the camera.

Below: If one motor's good, two must be better, right? The owner of this T bucket obviously thought so, building the car with a severely stretched wheelbase in order to fit in a pair of small-block Chevies. The hard part about running twin mills is connecting the two to run together, but this guy obviously figured it out as it's on the street.

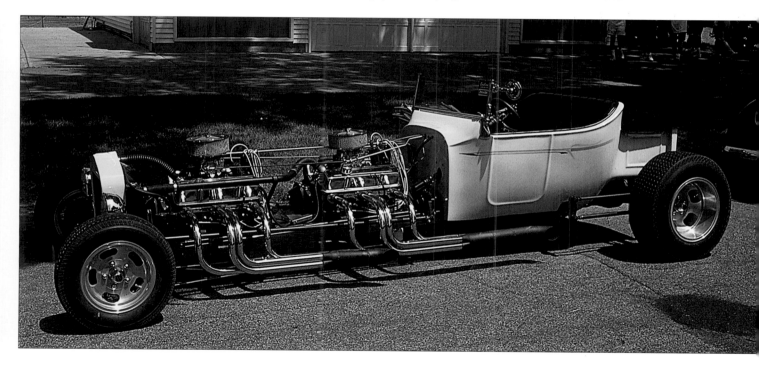

Classic Profile: *1932 THREE WINDOW*

Though not a famous car, Randy Ramey's '32 three window typifies the way billet aluminum was employed in rods during the 1980s—albeit usually not as well executed as seen here. Bob Reid milled all the ally seen in the interior, as well as plenty on the exterior, including the wheels, before it was red anodized and certain parts milled or drilled again to achieve a two-tone effect. The car was certainly no smoothy like those coming out of Hot Rods by Boyd for instance, with its chromed door hinges, stock lights, bumpers, and other trim, but it marked a trend towards more high-tech interiors and one-off trim parts.

Right: The Pompano Trim Shop upholstered the interior, including the headliner, to match the Recaro seats bolted directly to the floor. This allowed a reasonable amount of headroom in the chopped cabin. A chromed rollbar behind the seats offers some crash protection.

Below: Starting with an original body and chassis, 120 coats of paint went on to get this finish, but not before the roof came down 4½in in the front and 3½in in the rear. A 331ci Chevy V8 lives under the three piece hood, fed by a trio of Rochester carbs with nitrous oxide, and water injection. A 9in Ford axle helps put the power down, with an independent set-up under the front end.

Above: You'd think with a woody there'd be enough room for the luggage! Actually, we suspect the trailer is purely hauled because it looks cool, with fenders and wheels to match those on the '38 Ford—even the tonneau matches the roof on the wagon.

Left: No, Anglia fans, Ford never built a coupe version; this is the handiwork of Kevin Pittam riding high on an I beam axle and leaf springs, and powered by an aluminum 215ci Buick V8.

Above: In case you were wondering, the roof is hinged at the rear for passenger access. A 6-71 GMC blown Pontiac 289ci V8 powers this low '23T, running an 8in dropped Morris I beam front axle.

Opposite: A former B/Gas Supercharged drag racer, this strip refugee still retains its old race car looks, from the stance to the Cal Automotive five-piece fiberglass front end. The old hemi is long gone though—a 454 big-block Chevy and Turbo 400 trans now residing between the boxed frame rails.

Above: Not far removed from the Altereds on the dragstrip in appearance or horsepower, dropping a blown hemi into a T bucket is definitely overkill, but nothing can beat it for looks. The chopped windshield and roof just add to the cartoonish appearance, while the brass and gold plating lend a classy look.

Left: Pete Lattner's '35 Ford sedan gets its motivation from a 1977 351ci Ford V8 and Mustang four-speed transmission. He has owned the two door since 1965, which goes some way to explaining the Olds rear end on parallel leaf springs and particularly the '61 Pontiac tempest front clip with '69 Chevy discs and spindles. There are Sunflower yellow rod rolls on Western wheels.

Opposite: Built as a show car in 1983, this unchopped but channeled '34 coupe featured Jaguar independent rear suspension, homebrewed independent front, and ZZ Top-inspired graphics. An Inglese induction system with four IDA Weber carbs fed a small-block Chevy.

Classic Profile: *JAMIE MUSSELMAN'S '33*

Boyd Coddington and his contemporaries made the high-tech billet look popular in the '80s, the Vern Luce coupe leading the way. However, by virtue of it being a roadster, Jamie Musselman's similar '33 was eligible to win the AMBR trophy, which it did in '82. It was Coddington's first AMBR winner and wore the first set of Boyd's wheels. These two rods were probably most responsible for the popularity of this look throughout the '80s, which was like a breath of fresh air at the time, the hobby perfectly placed for such a new direction. With names such as Steve Davis, Dan Fink, Terry Hegmann, Thom Taylor, Art Chrisman, Vic Kitchens, John Buttera, and Boyd Coddington involved, the Musselman '33 couldn't fail to impress.

Opposite: Longtime rodder Art Chrisman was responsible for building the four Weber-equipped 355ci Chevy in the '33, backed by a Doug Nash five speed. Hot Rods by Boyd scratch-built the frame and independent chrome moly suspensions, while the three-piece 2024 billet aluminum wheels were the forerunners of the Boyd's Wheels empire.

Opposite: Somewhere in among building three versions of his famous black and flamed roadster, *Street Rodder* magazine founder Tom McMullen found time late in the decade to build Tom's Tub—a two-door '32 phaeton, flamed of course, and with that distinctive grille insert.

Right: As well as billet, this was the decade of the phantom—rods built to look as though they came from the factory that way, despite never having been offered. Gary Vahling put together this '46 phantom roadster pick-up from a Ford sedan and F1 truck rear fenders, yet to the uninitiated it looks as though Ford built it that way. Mission accomplished!

Above: Daring to be different didn't always work. This stretched high-tech '33/'34 coupe runs full rear fenders but none on the front, square headlights, and is fully channeled, though the jury's still out on that Porsche 911 whaletail on the decklid…

Opposite: This early Willys has been roadster-ized and Pro Streeted, with strut front suspension top mounts poking through the hood sides. Side-opening hood and trunk converted to a rumble seat are unusual features, while the owner obviously doesn't feel the need to add headlights to his ride.

Right: A '30/'31 Model A tub sits on a '32 chassis with the horns removed front and rear for a cleaner look. Four bar suspension at each corner ensures a smooth ride, and the red and white scalloped paint scheme harks back to Gee Bee airplanes and lakes racing hot rods of decades past.

Opposite: When is a roadster not a roadster? When it's a cabriolet. Fixed windshield posts and wind-up windows make it so, necessitating a unique shape to the folding roof, too. Gorgeous paint is perfectly complemented by chrome wire wheels, large stock headlights, and bumpers.

Left: Orange Twist brought home the AMBR trophy for Ermie Immerso in 1988, an Ardun equipped flathead V8 behind the grille of the full fendered 'Deuce roadster. With nerf bars, hairpin radius rods, and halibrands, this is so far the only retro rod to win the trophy.

Below: Fully trim-bedecked 1948 Chevy Fleetline doesn't need anything bodywise to make it stand out, though this one has had a running gear transplant, and been dropped in the weeds—at the front at least. The resulting rake says this is a hot rod rather than a lowrider, as the Chevy makes excellent base material for both.

Right: Popular in the '60s as base material for gassers, the little English Austin Devons, and their two door brother the Dorset, now make fine street rods. Funny how they all seem to have been manufactured in '48 though! This example runs Centerline Champ 500 wheels and a somewhat rearward driving position.

Above: A low red rod with a tan leather interior—we're definitely in the '80s here, yet though this '32 phaeton has the stance, solid hood sides, billet windshield posts, and four bar suspension, the wire wheels, bumpers, and running boards keep it from being too high tech. The quality of panel fit is superb here, difficult to achieve on a four-door open car with all the associated body flex.

Classic Profile: *VICKY BY BOYD*

Hotelier Carl Katerjian's '32 Victoria is instantly recognizable as a Boyd-built car, finished as it is in Boyd Red and wearing 14x6 and 15x8in Boyds Wheels. However, by now most of the work was being done in-house at Hot Rods by Boyd—such as the chassis and bodywork. The company had found a formula, and there were plenty of customers willing to pay for a car built that way and with that look. Boyd was responsible for putting many fantastic cars into the hobby before the bubble burst on his empire in later years.

Right: The 1½in chop is subtle, yet noticeable, but how many spotted the 2in sectioned grille shell, which results in a nice tapering effect to the bodywork as it comes forward? The almost compulsory small block Chevy and TH350 lies under the hood, with Weber induction.

Above: Under the rear there's a Boyd-built independent set-up, with JFZ brakes and coilover shock absorbers, plus plenty of red anodizing. The Independent front suspension was also built in-house to match.

Right: More red anodizing is evident inside the '32, the steering column topped by a Le Carra wheel, and the shifter dipped to match the column and gauge cluster. Sculptured door panels in magnolia match the seats.

Left: Using a quad camshaft Ferrari V12, Roy Brizio built this super low stretched '32 roadster for Jim Ells, taking the AMBR trophy in.1987. The rod featured a one-off chassis and V'd windshield, plus a three-piece hood and horizontal bars in the grille insert. No trailer queen, this roadster has covered many road miles since.

Opposite: As well as the high-tech and Pro Street trends, Fat Attack became popular by mid-decade—this '39 convertible combining the latter and smooth looks. The trend became so big that aftermarket body manufacturers such as Gibbon Fiberglass tooled up to laminate what had until recently been unpopular body styles.

Left: COE, or cab over engine, trucks became popular in all sorts of configurations, whether flatbeds, ramp trucks, tilt beds, with additional camper shells, and more. Most opted to mount the motor behind the cab though, such as the blown big block in this example. Here we see large single Mickey Thompson rear tires, though some have twin rear wheels.

Opposite: In a mix of styles which shouldn't work but does, this high back 1915 T bucket has a track nose with aluminum aerofoils, matching the huge wing at the rear. Finned covers hide the front disc brakes and mount the calipers.

Right: This repro retro Deuce hiboy hit the streets in '85, with an aluminum 215ci Buick V8 in the handmade chassis rails complete with characteristic swage line.

Above: Model A hiboy may have a 59A-B flathead V8, but under the floor there's a C4 auto trans, open driveshaft and 9in axle for reliability.

Opposite: This should go some way to explaining why the '40 Ford makes such a cool hot rod. Drop the front, add exhaust cutouts behind the front wheel, and you're halfway there.

Left: This '37 Ford two-door sedan is an ex-magazine project car, with the heavy chop executed by Paul Wayling, who removed the drip rails at the same time.

Opposite: If you owned a rare real steel '32 Ford Victoria, you'd think twice about making any drastic body modifications, but why would you want to, with a body shape this nice? Half chromed wires and lowered stance are the only deviations from stock bodywise. Oh, and the red paint.

Below: Here's an example of hot rod evolution. Check out this perfectly nice '34 coupe street rod, then turn to page 342 and see what it became ten years later. Believe it or not it's the same car, though back in the '80s it was somewhat more sedate, with stock grille and original size three piece hood.

Classic Profile: CLUB SPORT COUPE

Pennsylvania-based rod shop Posies built this 1932 Ford Club Sport Coupe and wowed the troops on its debut. From its cantilevered hood which hinged up and over the grille shell to the two-plus-two styled faux soft top roof, from the Rolls Royce-like plush woodgrained interior to the unique graphics, it was a '32 like no other. Renowned for pushing the envelope with his personal and customer projects, it was but the latest in a line of distinctive rods from Ken Fenical, aka Posies— a line which continues to this day.

Right: Not your usual street rod interior for sure! Okay so there's a tilt column and three-spoke 'wheel, but a woodgrained '32 dash and lower panels? The luxury two-plus-two cabin featured passenger seats in the rear, yet felt like a three window to drive.

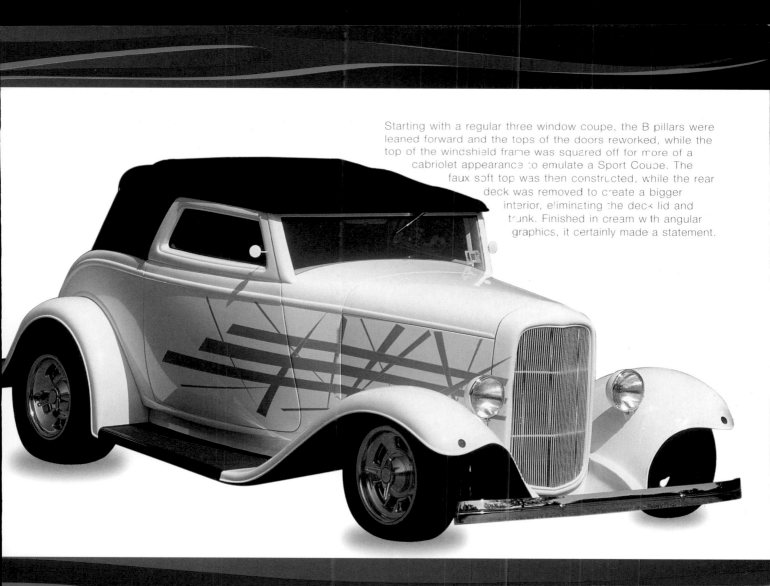

Starting with a regular three window coupe, the B pillars were leaned forward and the tops of the doors reworked, while the top of the windshield frame was squared off for more of a cabriolet appearance to emulate a Sport Coupe. The faux soft top was then constructed, while the rear deck was removed to create a bigger interior, eliminating the deck lid and trunk. Finished in cream with angular graphics, it certainly made a statement.

Left: Owner-built street rods rarely look this great, but Geoff Cousins undertook all the fabrication and machine work on his '34, from the unique front suspension, including the uprights and spindles, to the wheel centers and genuine knock-offs. The small block is fed by a quartet of downdraught Webers, the power leading to a Cousins-built independent rear.

Opposite: Though now in perfect condition, with a one piece flip front and opening windshield, Bob Jeffries' Fordson—or Thames van—was certainly rough when found, with even the roof panel rotten. Now with a V8, independent front suspension, and a four bar rear squeezed into its tiny proportions, it lives once more as a street rod.

6

1990s and beyond

After the explosion of different trends and ideas that occurred in the '80s, anything seemed to go by the time the '90s rolled along. Ever more outrageous phantoms, complete scratch-built bodies from super-talented craftsmen, and stretched and tweaked versions of age-old favorites all became popular. The advent of increasingly larger wheel sizes brought new challenges for the high-tech guys, while at the other end of the scale the nostalgia scene went from strength to strength, as did the arrival of another facet of the hobby, that of restoring old hot rods.

Left: Quad Dellorto carbs feed a 388ci Chevy in this Gibbon-bodied fiberglass '37 Ford Club Cabriolet. Pete & Jakes parts were used throughout the chassis build-up.

Above: After a few years break from car building, and having been involved with trikes for a while before that, Ed "Big Daddy" Roth returned with a modern version of the Beatnik Bandit, Bandit II, in typically flamboyant style.

Right: Phil Rutherford's '33 roadster was originally built as a full fendered street rod, but soon morphed into a circuit racer style rod. The front cycle fenders are almost molded around the tires and fit so closely you have to do a double take.

Below: Full fendered Model As had rarely looked as good as this—or as low. In fact, with the tires filling the fenderwells and minimal clearance between the two, it couldn't get any lower. The doors on this '28 have been flush fitted.

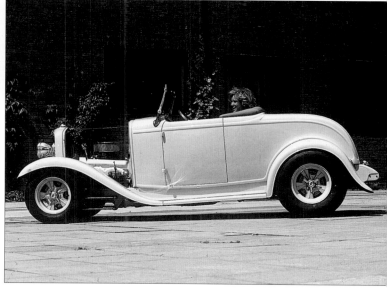

Left: Looking for an alternative powerplant for a street rod gets harder and harder. How about a Caddy Northstar motor, still relatively uncommon, or even a Toyota baby hemi V8? Colin Ayers went several steps further by installing a 380ci '67 Rolls Royce V8 in his Deuce coupe. Owning a Rolls Royce garage came in handy no doubt, while the lack of engine mounts on the side of the block (it's mounted front and rear) made routing headers a breeze.

Opposite: With a body fabricated from scratch in steel by Dave Palmer, Barry Flood's 38in stretched phantom Model A pick-up finished up with a wheelbase of 140in in 1995. Power came from a 302ci Ford V8, transferred through a C6 trans to a fully detailed Jaguar IRS.

Right: A simple touch such as the color coded rims on the rare Radir wheels ensure this '32 will stand out in a crowd, even if the rest of the rod is nothing particularly outstanding. Peach paint, neat stance, and a color matched small-block Chevy all add up to a very nice package, however.

Below: Wide whites on polished five spokes and matching scallops are sure attention grabbers for this Model A Tudor. The chopped top enforces the image of an up-to-date but slightly retro street rod. The tires, wheels, and paint detailing are different enough from the norm to ensure this rod received plenty of magazine ink when it first appeared.

Opposite: The advent of more and better quality reproduction bodies made street rodding more accessible, especially as some were offered in almost kit form. This beautifully finished '29 coupe has a V6 Ford for power, which fits the small A engine bay perfectly, and an independent front end with a steering rack hidden behind the extended front apron.

Classic Profile: *MCMULLEN ROADSTER*

1991 saw the debut of the final part of Tom McMullen's roadster trilogy. The first '32 was bought in the late '50s and modified into the '60s; the second version with IFS was built in '76, and by the early '90s, Tom was unable to resist the urge to build "the ultimate hiboy." Starting with a TCI frame and Wescott's body, the project was kept deliberately as close to the original car as possible, though as it had been continuously evolving, Tom had to choose a particular era to recreate, settling on the 1964 version of the car, with drilled I beam and 'bones, parachute, Halibrand wheels, and Moon tank out front.

Right: With Goodyear rubber all round on polished Halibrands, slicks on the rear naturally, and flames, and pinstriping recreating Ed Roth's originals as closely as possible.

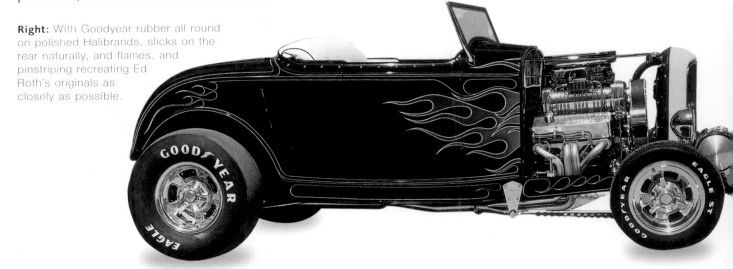

Left: The black and white Naugahyde interior was stitched by Darryll "Whitey' Morgan, who stitched the interior in the original car, with a dash stuffed full of Classic gauges, again as per the original. A LeCarra steering wheel turns a '56 F100 box, and Dan Fink Metalworks supplied the windshield, and posts. The black wool carpet is edged in white for authenticity, and Tom undertook the wiring himself, a task for which he is famed.

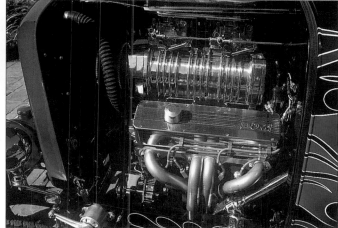

Right: The LT 1 Chevy small block was fitted with cc'd E&M heads and TRW pistons, with a B&M cam, suitable for the B&M Megablower with twin Edelbrock 600cfm carbs. A Hurst shifter operated a Doug Nash five speed connected to the engine via a McLeod clutch. The motor kicked out 550hp at 7,000rpm with the blower overdriven by 20%. The HPC coated headers were fabricated by Mike Hamm.

Right: Magenta scallops over yellow paint will get you noticed, but then those huge Weld wheels and Mickey Thompson tires out back aren't exactly subtle. This Pro Street '33 three window coupe has been completely smoothed from the door handles and hinges to the hood hardware and side louvers—the latter replaced with simple reverse scoops.

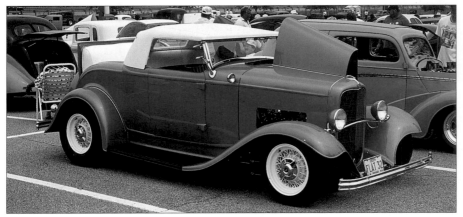

Opposite: There's a definite '50s flavor to this full fendered and flamed '34 five window. The hoodless rod shows off its flathead and beehive oil filter, while the nerf bars and Merc hubcaps don't hurt one bit.

Left: This subtle and tasteful full fendered '32 uses old time tricks like the molded door hinges and dropped headlight bar, but has modern style cutouts in the hood sides to show off the detailed flathead V8. A neat touch is the blue and white color scheme carried through to the interior and roof.

Opposite: Not so much a '36 two-door phaeton as a two-door sedan with the roof hacked off! You can still see where he side window frames start to curve up into the pillars. Seaweed style flames cover the orange paint and Moon discs cover the wheels, but what's going to cover the driver if it rains? Hope they packed a good coat!

Below: This unchopped '33 three window has strange proportions once channeled and with a stretched nose. Chromed split wishbones suggest an earlier build, though the widened McClean wires and matching tires on the rear are definitely more recent additions

Below: "Chopped 'n' channeled" was once the ultimate for any hot rod, but the reality is that you just don't see too many rods built that way. And for good reason, as it translates into a very cramped cabin. This '28 A coupe is built that way, however, with a tri-power equipped mouse motor and outside headers. An opening windshield is almost a necessity on a rod such as this, as it gets awful warm inside.

Left: Who says flames have to be red and orange over black? The flames on this '33 hiboy roadster continue down onto the chassis rails making everything at the front of the car red, including the grille and headlight buckets.

Above: Judy Hodges from Tennessee chose a Total Performance chassis and Wescotts body for her version of the classic deuce roadster, adding a 9in rear, buggy sprung front and 350ci Chevy V8. Bobby Griffey upholstered the rod in oxblood leather.

Opposite: Another rod that suggests an earlier build. Possibly even an ex-race car if the spaceframe chassis is anything to go by, this blown hemi T with twin Predator carbs and Centerline wheels looks like a heap of fun.

Above: Super swoopy chopped '34 five window features heavily modified widened fenders and cutouts in the hood side panels. The four downdraught carbs poke through the hood, while monster meats are stuffed under the rear.

Opposite: It's difficult to come up with an unusual twist on the decades-old flame treatment, but this guy did it with his '34, keeping them solely on the doors and hood sides, creating a neat "reverse flame" at the front edge. It had probably been thought of before, as all the best ideas are, but never as well executed.

Right: Pick-ups make great nostalgia rods, as this hemi-fied '32 Ford attests. Retro down to its wishbones and plugged caps, it's one cool hauler.

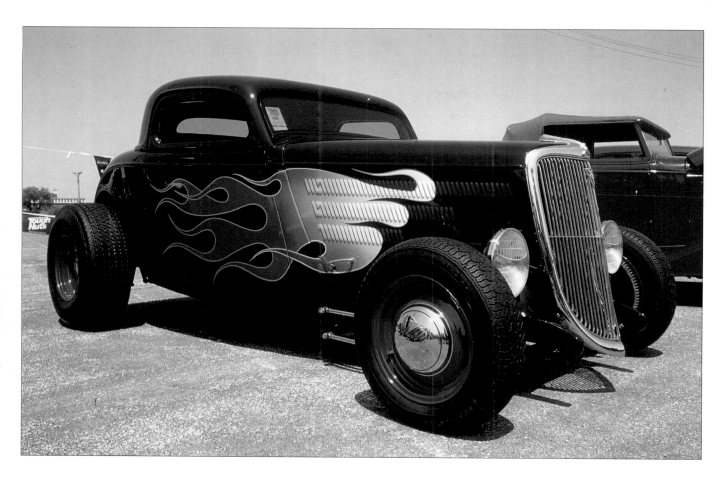

Classic Profile: PRO STREET ANGLIA

The gasser racers of the '60s attracted small, light cars in which to drop large powerful engines, and in addition to cars such as '33 and '40/'41 Willys, Crosleys, Henry Js, and the like, English imports in the shape of Ford Anglias and Prefects, Austin Devons, and European Simcas and Fiats were perfect for the task. While the drags claimed a few, many of today's survivors can be found cruising fairgrounds as street rods.

Right: Bobby Burks' Anglia wasn't an ex-race car, as he found the stocker sitting in a field quietly rusting away. With a narrowed, boxed and C'd original frame, it began a new lease of life with a 9in rear axle on Aldan coilovers, and a narrowed TCI front suspension with '37 Ford spindles and late Ford disc brakes. Weld wheels are at each corner shod with Mickey Thompson tires.

Above: The recessed firewall gives an indication of just how small an Anglia engine bay is, but Bobby neatly installed a 350ci Chevy, detailed in cream to contrast with the Porsche red bodywork.

Right: Though the outer bodywork is stock, the dash has been replaced with a custom-made item, the only painted part of the interior. A tilt column, woodrim wheel, and B&M shifter take up most of the rest of the cabin in this narrow car.

Right: Mopars can make neat rods—just try making a case against this '34 Dodge pick-up. Beautiful execution with a great two-tone paint job which incorporates scallops on the hood, and the use of chromed wire wheels make this truck a standout. With a slight nose-down stance, it's hit the nail right on the head in the looks department.

Opposite: Rodded by Stewart Revill in the '70s and constantly updated since, this is the mid-'90s version with a Volvo rear axle replacing the Jaguar IRS, complete with self levelling system poached from a GM sedan. A Jag IFS still supports the front end, now home to a Chevy V8 which replaces the Buick motor previously fitted to this Austin.

Right: How stock can a car be yet still be classed as a hot rod? Ask Chris Rawlins, whose Model B phaeton is stock, apart from a chopped windshield and smaller diameter wire wheels. This way he can attend restorer meets, as well as rod runs, and enjoy both.

Left: Stock height three window '32s must be pretty rare as most seem to be chopped, but here's one that came through unscathed, almost but not quite managing the smooth look, with a few extraneous protrusions spoiling the red coachwork.

Left: How many rodders started their hobby career behind the wheel of a '39 or '40 Ford? Ah, but was yours a red hot rod coupe with chrome reverse rims? The cowl vent of this '39 is open to grab some much needed cool air.

Below: Dennis Varni's '29 hiboy made the cover of *Rod & Custom* in 1971, then 21 years later, after an extensive rebuild, scooped the AMBR trophy at Oakland. No sooner had it won, than Varni was out driving the wheels off it across the country.

Left: Okay, it's guess the base vehicle time. Whatever it started as, probably a Studebaker, this cool kustom pick-up now employs two pairs of Packard taillights butted end to end, canted headlights, and a custom grille, as well as a healthy roof chop and moulded front end.

Above: Another ex-drag racer, this '41 Willys was actually rolled on the strip and extensively damaged, but resurfaced as a Pro Street street rod in the 1990s. The blown 426 Chrysler hemi was long gone, a big-block Chevy now powering the very low coupe.

Above: It's not the flames that appear to exit from the lakes style headers that is the trick part of this '32, it's the roof that folds away into the hinged rear deck that has rodders gawping wherever it's parked.

Right: This four door '34 is the handiwork of Greg Saunders of Florida. The DuPont Seafoam Green sedan features stainless steel four bar suspended 9in and chromed I beam axles, with Boyds wheels all round.

Below: Chopped and Carson-topped '36 Ford cabriolet custom runs fender skirts and a Continental kit laid down at the same angle as the rear panel. Flipper hubcaps, Briz bumper, solid hood sides, and re-worked grille all aid the appearance of this taildragger

Left: Not all rods are weekend-only rides, as this '40 Ford pick-up proves. Spotted in a southern California parking lot the truck is used as a daily business vehicle, probably providing more fun and looked after better than any new truck would.

Opposite: Lance Scorchik used to do the illustrations for *Rod Action* magazine, and his personal rides reflect the same cartoon-like approach to rodding as his drawings. Heavily slant chopped with a laid-back windshield, low mounted headlights, and outrageous big 'n' littles, his Jersey Suede '34 is a cartoon rod come to life.

Right: Notice something not quite right about this Model A roadster? If you're wondering why the doors are too long and the rear quarters too short, it's because this particular roadster started life as a Sport Coupe, the door tops and windshield coming off to form a roadster. The nostalgia rod runs a tri-carbed flathead linked to a modern five speed.

Classic Profile: GOLDEN STAR

Irmie Immerso's Golden Star won the AMBR trophy in '89, but this is the revamped version which came back and repeated the feat in '91. Not content with winning at Oakland, he sent the car and its display on a nationwide tour to win the ISCA championship as well. The 1925 T was displayed on a rotating angled turntable surrounded by lights—an elaborate display which took hours to assemble. Immerso is the only car owner to win the AMBR three times. Built by Don Thelan, Golden Star featured a rare Ford Indy motor with twin camshafts on each bank of the V8, and a gold plated induction system. In fact, gold plating was used extensively throughout the track-nosed, turtle-decked T.

Golden Star was painted in candy tangerine, including the cam covers on the quad cam Ford mill. Irmie still has the car in his collection and showed it again at the 50th anniversary of the Oakland Roadster Show.

Left: This fully accessorized '47 Pontiac may be classed as a lowrider but deserves a second look. Whereas rodders remove most trim and unnecessary adornments, lowricers like to add as many as possible, from the sunvisor and vintage window mounted air conditioner to the Appleton spotlights and factory accessory lights on the front. Gold plating and McClean 60-spoke wires with skinny crossplies further add to the image.

Above: Even odd-rod fans may have trouble identifying this one. Try the 1937 Vauxhall Ten. Dave Rothwell extensively modified the ex-four door, the suicide front doors now converted to hidden hinges. A Mercedes gave up its roof section complete with sunroof, while Ford independent front suspension was narrowed to fit. No surprise under the hood—it's a small-block Chevy.

Above: Originally rodded in 1958 with a Caddy 331ci mill, this '32 three window has led an exciting life yet never succumbed to the hacksaw, even though the original firewall has long gone. Nowadays, a Chevy V8 pushes the coupe along, occupants sitting comfortably in the oxblood leather tuck 'n' roll interior.

Opposite: Compare this picture of an English-bodied Model B sedan and you'll see it's more angular than its American counterpart, with suicide doors that have a straight front edge as opposed to curved. It also proves the Brits know what makes a neat hot rod, with polished Halibrands, drilled I beam, and Moon tank among other neat parts.

Above: You can't even say "If it's unchopped it must be steel" any longer, with stock height '32 coupes available in fiberglass, though this one's the real deal, with a panhard rod controlling lateral movement of the dropped tube axle.

Opposite: Originally belonging to a doctor in Scotland when delivered new, this bodily unmolested '32 five window has been sympathetically rodded, the red lower half letting any enquirer know it's no stocker.

Left: With hairpin front and strangely braced split wishbone rear suspension, this tri-power equipped Model B has a nostalgic look, though with disc brakes at the front.

Above: Stretched 8in in the front, Swedish tattoo artist Ove Skoog's '34 coupe is loosely based on old fighter plane nose art designs. The teeth in the grille sheet actually open and close with the temperature of the engine, while above a '37 headlight bucket protrudes from the blanked off upper grille.

Left: With a 2½in roof chop and filled roof panel, this '32 sedan is all steel and sits on an original chassis, though updated with an 8in Mustang rear axle and dropped I beam with Posies spring and Jaguar disc brakes. Power is supplied by a 350/350 Chevy combination, the rod rolling on Solids wheels.

Below: This '34 roadster is all Ford, from its 302 and C4 to its 8in rear axle on parallel leaf springs. The front suspension is all home-brewed stainless steel tubular A arms, though using Ford spincles and based on Ford geometry. Even the paint is a Ford color, Radiant Red!

Above: Sweden has a strong nostalgia scene running alongside the more mainstream events, with rod runs strictly for older style rods, customs, and bikes.

Opposite: Roy Brizio went all '60s with this gold Deuce coupe with white running boards. Mercury capped chrome rims complemented the stock appearing body.

Right: These three early-style Flathead-powered '27Ts, two V8 and one four-banger, belong to East Coast Sidewinder members—the east coast of England!

Below: Hand-formed from aluminum by Al Stevens with a full bellypan, Jim Pantall's track nosed A roadster runs a Riley four banger under the hood and no screen. With the seating set low inside the perimeter of the frame rails, it eliminates the usual look of sitting way too high in an A.

Opposite: Anglias make great little street rods—take a look at this stunning example in pearl blue. With independent suspension at all four corners, and a Daimler hemi providing go, aided by a Wade blower, you can bet that acceleration is brisk, along with go-kart handling.

Right: Two-tone black and green really suits Bob Holland's '35 Chevy pick-up truck. Sitting low over polished five spokes, this truck racked up many miles under Bob's ownership before being sold on abroad to Europe in the late 1990s.

Left: This neat 1940 Mercury convertible is obviously a crowd pleaser, and a combination of slammed stance, red interior, arrow straight black paintwork, and traditional flames is hard to beat. More licks around the rear fenderwells would do the trick, though!

Below: With the full fendered '27T's popularity on the dragstrips, it was only a matter of time before one was put on the street. This Brogie-style street rod has all the race car accoutrements—cage, large diameter header collector—but is it a fairground cruiser or legitimate street rod?

Right: The spec list for Stuart Loeber's A roadster reads like a nostalgia rodder's wish list: Halibrand quick change, Model A spring, '32 rails, Buick finned drums, F100 steering box, 4in crank flathead, four 97s on a Sharp intake, Granatelli Corporation heads, and Super bell I beam.

Opposite: A TCI frame and aftermarket '30/'31 A pick-up cab provided the basis for this truck project, a Ford 351ci Cleveland motor providing more than enough power to propel the lightweight rod to decidedly illegal speeds, aided by a hi-rise Ford Motorsport intake, and 600cfm Holley carb.

Right: There's not a whole lot of room left inside a channeled A coupe, especially one that has a recessed firewall to accommodate a built flathead V8 in the stock wheelbase A chassis. Chop the roof as well and you're just asking for back problems!

Classic Profile: *CUSTOM PACKARD*

Doug Thompson built this 1946 Packard Clipper for Missouri's Richard Ratty, debuting it in 1990. Hundreds if not thousands of man hours went into the reconstruction of a Packard like no other. Probably the most noticeable modification is the way Thompson dropped the side windows below the car's waistline after performing the heavy roof chop, for a unique look. Chopping the rear of the roof more than the front also gave the Packard a fastback style.

Right: Joe Poindexter of Kansas City retrimmed the Packard in magnolia leather with brown carpets. The late model steering with column shifter was topped by a LeCarra 'wheel to retain an older appearance.

Left: A subtle but very time consuming modification was the addition of the peak across the roof and down to the rear bumper. The fenders were pulled back and Lincoln headlight buckets added before the Clipper was coated in Midnight Plum.

Below: Budget hot rod building at its best. Joe Paynter used parts from all sorts of unlikely places, such as a Volvo for the four banger to bring his '27T in under budget. And what a budget—just $1,500 in 1998!

Above: Built by a coachbuilder you won't be surprised to find this '27T was hand painted, but try to find any brushmarks! Homebuilt Du Vall style screen and use of a tri-carbed six pot make it stand out.

Opposite: The frame for Rich Llewellin's Deuce roadster began life under a Model B tractor found on a golf course, but is now part of a cool hot rod, with magnesium spindle mount 12 spokes and a tri-power equipped 283ci 'vette small block.

Right: Smoothed off and color keyed, the only brightwork on this '37 Club Cabriolet is the wheels. The smooth look even extended to the windshield, which was bonded with a narrow rubber seal around its perimeter, and V-butted in the centre, eliminating the rubber strip. Though removable in theory, most Carson tops stayed firmly secured to the vehicle.

Opposite: John Carambia bolted this four banger powered '29 Model A together from a pile of parts in just ten days, modifying and pinching the '32 frame at the firewall to accept the earlier body. The primered sheetmetal contrasts with the apple green wires.

Above: Almost too smooth, this '34 cabriolet snows the way many street rods went in the '90s, with even steel bodies massaged to within an inch of their lives and ending up looking like fiberglass ones. Pastel colors didn't help, but t was a popular look at the time.

Right: If you've an impression to make, mount a blown big-block Chevy in your ride and call the job done! The owner of this suicide-doored and alligator-hooded Chevy pick-up has done just that, adding Pro Street rubber to the rear for good measure.

Opposite: The modifications to this '46 Ford coupe are endless: chopped roof with drip rails removed, molded fenders and running boards, radiused door corners, frenched lights, filled seams, bonded and butted glass, custom front pan, detrimmed, handles removed... and that's just the bodywork!

Right: Taking the term "smooth" to new levels, this '33 coupe has been finished—unusually—in white, a clinical color suited to showing off the minimalist exterior of this street rod. Big chrome headlights and wheels are the only let-up from the white-out.

Above: Lose the wide rear wheels, and front four bar, and this would be a great period hot rod. But has it been modified or is it an almost-correct new build? The front wheels and tires, generator-equipped dressed flathead, and DuVall screen suggest an older car updated, but only the owner knows for sure...

Opposite: If you want to be seen, paint your truck lime green! Adding orange steels and caps wouldn't hurt either, then park in front of something unusual to guarantee photographers catch your ride. This chopped Ford has had the hood extended to include the top part of the grille shell.

Below: Model A sedans are always cool, and even cooler with a vintage portable air conditioning unit hanging off a side window. Simple in the extreme, fill these babies with ice and the air passing through them will enter the car cooler. Whether they're any benefit while cruising fairgrounds at walking pace is debatable, but they can't be beaten for looks. With the sun shining through that glass panel in the roof, we'll bet the occupants of this particular A need all the help they can get staying chilled.

Left: Yellow steels wrapped in whitewall crossplies look good against the black paintwork of this '32 roadster, caught out cruising aimlessly, though the nostalgia vibe is somewhat spoiled by the disc brakes on the front axle.

Opposite: The red and white pleated seat of this flamed '30/'31 A hiboy looks like a great place to be on a warm summer's evening, with the mellow burble of the flathead's exhaust accompanying its passage down the street.

Right: Green and yellow sounds like an awful combination on paper, but boy does it work in the flesh—and the whitewalls don't hurt either! This '40 coupe is going to remain seared onto the eyeballs of anyone who looks at it even briefly.

Above: Jack Buete's '34 Dodge pick-up is as sweet as they come, with a reproduction bed to smooth the lines, a filled roof, and the pièce de resistance, a 270ci Dodge Red Ram hemi bolted to a 1970s Dodge four speed, keeping it in the family.

Opposite: The American Bantam was a US-bodied English Austin, usually only seen in rodding circles as the bodies on dragsters, and occasional gassers. This one's complete though, and cute as a button as a street rod.

Left: Ever wondered how a '35 Ford five window coupe differed from a '36? Then study these two parked right next to each other. The sheet metal forward of the cowl and also the grille are the main differences.

Classic Profile: SMOOTHSTER

After winning the Ridler award in 1994 with his highly modified '37 Ford coupe dubbed Fatboy '37, for 1995 Fred Warren went several steps further. However, Smoothster didn't start out as his project, but was sold to him unfinished by Boyd Coddington, who in turn had purchased it from its instigator Robbie Midollo of New York state. Designed originally by Larry Erickson, well known metalworking master Graig Naff had been constructing the car. Though sold to Warren, the car was built at Boyd's, with further design input coming from Chip Foose during the build.

The hand-fabricated Art Deco grille was made from 66 separate brass bars to Erickson's original design, bevelled, block sanded, and chromed. Just-a-hobby rails formed the basis of the perimeter style chassis, with a '92 LT1 Corvette engine under the aluminum hood, the frame utilizing the Corvette's independent suspension front and rear, though not before it was all ground smooth and painted. Boyd used the unveiling of Smoothster to debut new 17 and 18in wheels, going by the same name as the car.

Right: Though based on a '37 Ford, the only stock parts used from that year's model on the final product were the headlights! The windshield is a cut down Corvette item joined at its top edge by a removable Carson-style hardtop. Reworked 'vette seats form the basis of the interior, ergonomically designed by Erickson, and upholstered in tan leather by Jim Griffin.

Right: In the mid '30s, Ford station wagons used maple framing and ribbing with passenger car front sheetmetal, but these wagons were, and still are, more commonly known as woodies. Today woodies are extremely desirable and expensive to restore. But there was a time in the '60s when they were unpopular and the surfers' transport of choice as they could accommodate boards, friends, and were cheap to buy. This '36 Ford woody has flawless black paintwork and is slammed over whitewall-shod steels for a perfect look.

Opposite: Designed by Thom Taylor and in association with Ford Motorsports, Roy Brizio put together this '60s inspired Deuce roadster, with an SVO 302 motor but using twin Holleys instead of fuel injection. Chromed Mercury wheels and hubcaps provide a different appearance, as does the '95 Mustang metallic purple paint on the fiberglass body.

Left: This tall T sedan somehow manages to cram a 215ci Buick motor into the ridiculously small engine bay, wearing Chevy valve covers, and a Weber carb. Though the fenders are fiberglass, the steel body was hand fabricated based on measurements taken from a '27T doctor's coupe.

Right: This severely chopped and channeled '32 three window is mounted on an English Ford Pilot chassis, a sedan very similar to a '36 Ford, which explains why the engine and radiator are mounted so far forward as they occupy their stock positions in the frame. This rod met an untimely end when a Range Rover turned across the street, T-boning the coupe in the driver's door. The substantial chassis saved the occupants' lives, though wrecking the rod beyond repair.

Opposite: A nostalgic turtle-decked T bucket uses a straight six Ford engine and four speed trans for power, with each seat either side of a high trans tunnel to enable the occupants to sit low in the body. This way the roof can be as low as it is. Split 'bones early Ford 16in wire wheels, and whitewalls perfect the early hot rod image.

Left: Nostalgia drag racing events have increased in popularity around the world. Here, the author tries his hand in his much-missed flathead-powered '28 A roadster, complete with nitrous oxide injection for this event in the mid '90s.

Below: A nicely detailed '32 wears a coat of satin black, yet is no low buck beater. The rumble seat means that the whole family can participate in both rod running and cruises, without having to sell the roadster.

Above: Nostalgia rods became big news with the younger rockabilly crowd during the late '80s and early '90s in England and Europe, rapidly gaining ground in the States not long after. This '34 coupe was pictured at England's Hemsby rock and roll weekender, regarded by many as the primo nostalgia rod show of the year.

Right: With the Austin hood emblem reproduced as a graphic down each side of the car, this Pro Street Austin Dorset makes a bold statement. Scant regard for scrub lines—where no part of the body or running gear should be below the bottom of each wheel rim to enable the car to still roll in a blowout—means the two door maintains a seriously low profile.

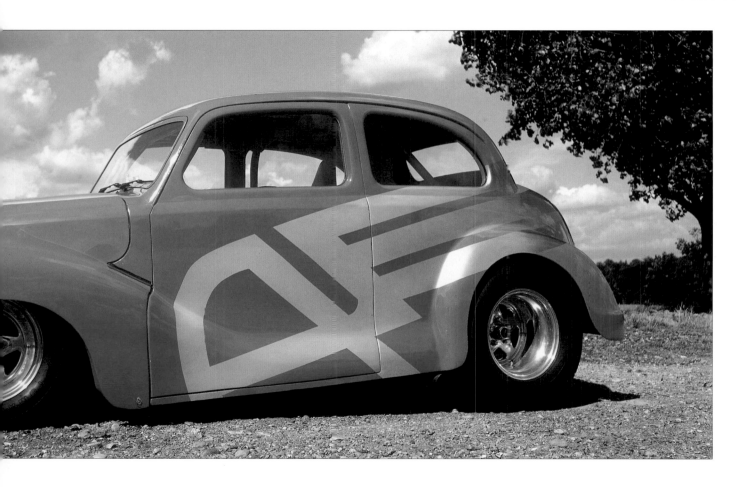

Opposite: Dutchman Perry van der Eertwegh's Pro Street two-door Willys sedan began as a four-door '38 with '40 front sheet metal. The doors were stretched 4¹/₂in to achieve the correct look, with the Hilborn scoop and carbs attached to a 6-71 blown 454ci Chevy poking through the hood.

Above: In a time when many '41 Willys coupes are fiberglass, Barry Grimes' street driven steel beauty not only looks the part but runs well too, picking up both front wheels on its way to ten second passes at nostalgia drag racing events.

Right: Is it a rod or custom? Who cares, this '37 Chevy Business Coupe is a great cruiser, updated with a straight six from a '75 Camaro in place of the old Stovebolt. It's packed full of speed equipment too, so it's no slouch out on the highway. A homemade 8in dropped axle brings the front down, with Posies 3in dropped springs and 2in blocks doing likewise at the rear.

Left: Nostalgia rods don't come much more period correct than Felix's '32. The V'd windshield, fully dressed flathead and hairpin radius rods go a long way to making you believe this is a genuine early hot rod, but the truth is that it was put together in the last decade of the century.

Below: You just don't see too many blown flathead V8s, and even when you do it's nearly always a SCoT blower or occasionally a Wade. So to see a GMC 6-71 atop Henry's finest is something of a shock, but here's one to prove it works. The '34 coupe it lives in is the perfect home for such madness.

Above: Ex-rod shop proprietor Steve Rain tools around in this cool T bucket with a small block Ford complete, with baffled zoomie headers. There's no brass on this baby, just chrome, and bright orange paint!

Opposite: To the uninitiated this '34 coupe could appear stock, though any hot rodder can tell it's modified. Under the unassuming grey exterior lies a 302ci Ford motor, 8in rear on coilovers, and homebrewed stainless steel IFS.

Right: Chuck Vranas' Lady Luck II gets its go-power from a big-block Chevy, and despite its show car appearance does see street action. Dedication-cum-clean-up time pays off when your car looks this clean. Hardtopped T is unusual but cool.

Below: You want flames? Check out this '46 Ford two-door sedan. The panels that aren't flamed are pinstriped. Painted matt black and slammed on the deck, Mexican blankets provide cheap upholstery, while the traditional licks covering most of the bodywork make sure this is a rod that gets noticed.

Right: There's plenty of work in this '41 Willys pick-up as the company never offered Fleetsides back then. This custom bed has been fabricated to flow with the curves of the original cab, even including the beltline. Running boards tie the body and bed together, with subtle rear fenders eliminating any slab-sided looks.

Classic Profile: *POSIES' EXTREMELINER*

Posies has been responsible for some of the most stunning street rods of the past 20 years, but with Extremeliner the rod and custom shop from Pennsylvania surpassed itself. Loosely based on a mix of '37 Ford and '37 Hispano-Suiza Xenia coupe, the faux woodie wagon featured many Art Deco touches on a Thom Taylor design, from cane and wicker used in the interior to the three bar design running through the project. Innovations abounded too, such as the front wheel covers which remained stationary when the car was in motion, and the specially made glass all round. The PPG paint was pretty special too, changing hue in different lights. Eight years under construction made it the biggest project Posies had tackled up to that point in time.

Right: A one-off steering wheel echoing the three bar design of the front wheel covers was manufactured for Extremeliner, while the interior is employing wicker, cane, and leather. With no actual dash, the VDO gauges are mounted below, the Vintage Air and Painless Wiring systems behind a bulkhead. A sound system by Alpine and Kicker features speakers behind wicker grilles either side of the cabin.

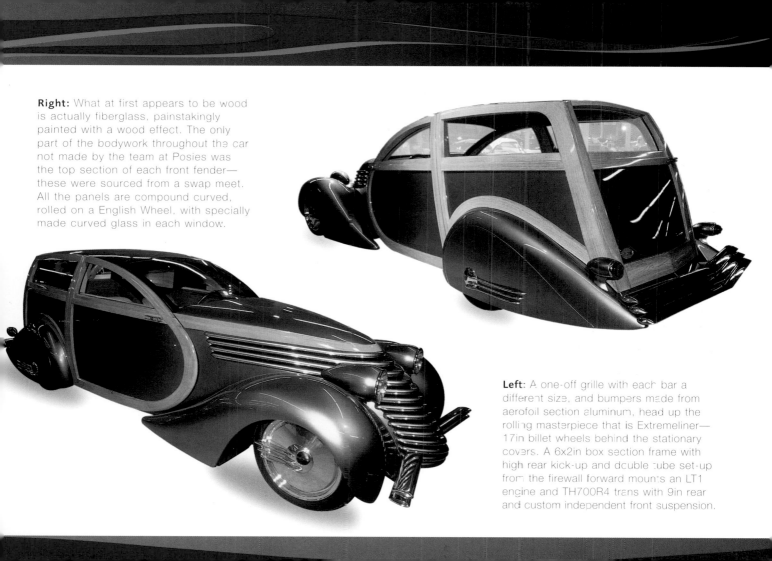

Right: What at first appears to be wood is actually fiberglass, painstakingly painted with a wood effect. The only part of the bodywork throughout the car not made by the team at Posies was the top section of each front fender— these were sourced from a swap meet. All the panels are compound curved, rolled on a English Wheel, with specially made curved glass in each window.

Left: A one-off grille with each bar a different size, and bumpers made from aerofoil section aluminum, head up the rolling masterpiece that is Extremeliner— 17in billet wheels behind the stationary covers. A 6x2in box section frame with high rear kick-up and double tube set-up from the firewall forward mounts an LT1 engine and TH700R4 trans with 9in rear and custom independent front suspension.

Opposite: Gary Keep's '34 coupe evolved gradually into the dual purpose street/strip machine pictured here. A 440ci Mopar V8 with Brodix heads took the '34 to a best quarter mile time of 10.69 without nitrous oxide, with the grille laid back, and the rear wheel wells moved up and out to accommodate 33x17x15 Firestone rubber.

Below: Pete Tyas' three window was channeled the width of the frame for a seriously low stance, a triple carbed aluminum headed ZZ4 Chevy delivering power to a Halibrand quick change with widened axle tubes and longer halfshafts required for the chrome reverse rims to clear the bodywork. This '32 personifies the show and go ethos—Tyas drove it everywhere.

Left: The voluminous hood of Ian Dawes' ex-four door '39 Willys hides a tunnel rammed 454 Chevy rat motor. Based on original boxed frame rails, the sedan featured a Jaguar third member with scratch-built stainless steel control arms and hub carriers, and a Fatman Fabrications IFS with TCI spindles. Wilwood brakes with polished aluminum calipers are used all round.

Opposite: The custom grille and '37 headlights on this '40 Ford pick-up contribute to altering the frontal appearance, while the top chop and two-tone paint broken up with graphics completes the transformation. Two-tone paint always used to have the darker color on the bottom, but in the '90s rodders started to swap them around.

Right: Wanting something to cause a stir racing against E-Type Jags, Healeys, and Aston Martins in historic circuit racing, Bernie Chodosh and Simon Lane decided on a '34 coupe. Weighing in at just 2,160lb, and with a built 327ci Chevy and T10 stickshift delivering 375-400bhp, the coupe was a terror on the straights but not so quick on the twisty bits.

Right: Hot rod overkill doesn't come much wilder than this blown Chrysler hemi-powered, heavily chopped, and tubbed '32 three window. With painted flames seemingly exiting from the capped lakes style headers, it's a surprise the driver doesn't have to wear a neck brace with the acceleration he must have available under his right foot!

Opposite: The list of body modifications on Sam Foose's '41 Ford convertible is a long one: molded fenders all round, custom rolled rear pan with frenched license plate, custom grille incorporating peak extending down from hood, chopped top, bonded and V-butted windshield, flush fitted headlights, and late model door mirrors, not to mention nosed, decked, and all trim and handles removed.

Below: With contemporary graphics dividing the two tone paint scheme, this '34 sedan featured independent suspension, billet wheels, and color keyed grille, and still looks fresh today.

Above: There will always be a place in street rodding for T buckets, though the "broken back" look of the '60s and '70s has given way to a slightly smoother look, with all the protuberances associated with such a car. The basic formula hasn't changed since the '50s though, and probably never will.

Right: A subtle exterior belies the potential in Gary McCormack's Thames delivery, the only hint coming from a glimpse of the rollcage through the windshield. A hot small block sends it down the road in a hurry.

Above: With a silver and black diamond pleated interior, and exterior appointments such as E/T 10 spokes and E/TIII wheels, Buick drums, and a DuVall windshield, you'd be forgiven for thinking this is just a nice street rod, but owner Lee Pike has seen 11 second timeslips from the 351 Cleveland powered '32 at nostalgia drag events.

Right: Just about as smooth as it's possible to get without going to a one-piece body with no windows, Frank Carroll's high-tech '34 employs plenty of red anodized billet, with everything not anodized painted red or covered in matching red leather.

Above: You'd never guess it now, but this '32 three window body came from an ex-stock car, and was about as beaten up as it could possibly be, with 3in holes cut into the rear corners of the roof and around the rear window, no returns around the decklid aperture, and no rear panel. Nowadays, it's restored to perfection, and sits on a Home Grown Hot Rods chassis rolling on polished Halibrands and super rare 16in Firestone dirt track tires in the rear.

Above: You want different, here it is! How about a Deuce roadster based on Toyota MR2 mechanicals, meaning a mid-engined layout with the gas tank under the hood where the engine would normally reside. A unique cantilevered independent front suspension put the coilover shocks inboard to clean up the lines on this very special '32.

Left: Carl Frith's Limefire-inspired '32 roadster beats to the tune of a Chrysler hemi fed by twin carbs. Though the rod runs a hood, this motor is worth showing off sometimes. Spindle mount Halibrands always look cool.

Below: Most of the pictures in this book are from the lens of Mike Key, and here's his '32 hiboy. Based on a new Brookville body, the all fresh steel roadster runs a Goodwrench 350 with tri-power, and kidney bean Halibrands.

Left: Caught on film at Roy Brizio's rodshop, the rollbar and harnesses are wise additions to this '34, considering the zoomie headered blown small-block behind the extended grille shell, covering a radiator big enough to cope with the cooling demands of such an engine.

Below: Built by Steve Moa for Tim Allen, this hard-formed track-nosed roadster is powered by a 351 Windsor Ford engine mated to a five speed stickshift, all mounted in a chrome moly tube frame. The brand new roadster harks back to earlier hot rodding times, with nostalgic parts such as the sprint car style steering and outside exhausts.

Opposite: Dave Cannon's award-winning Ford Pilot is an English body style that shares the cowl and front doors with a '36 Ford four door, and in fact the '36 front sheetmetal is interchangeable. The color coded bumpers and grille are contemporary, with running gear from a Jaguar XJ6 and a 327ci Chevy motor. Tan vinyl and leather cover the interior, incorporating seats from a Renault.

Classic Profile: SHOCKWAVE

Fred Warren had the honor of winning the AMBR trophy at the 50th anniversary Grand National Roadster Show with this totally unique roadster, Shockwave, just four years after winning with Smoothster. Starting with a Chip Foose design, the project got underway at Hot Rods by Boyd before transferring to California Street Rods when Boyd's closed. Marcel's Auto Metal was responsible for the gorgeous bodywork, which took over 1,000 hours to complete, with paint by Greg Morrell in candy tangerine.

Right: Paul Atkins Interiors in Alabama constructed the center console and seats, covering everything but the floor and dash in sand coloured leather. Johnny Anderson machined the billet steering wheel, while the Classic Instruments gauges were stripped and had their faces tinted body color. That's the kind of attention to detail required at AMBR level.

Below: The 17in Budnik wheels were manufactured to Chip Foose's design (with 20-inchers on the rear), with cross drilled and chromed Wilwood discs brakes and custom-machined billet aluminum A arm suspension. Dan Fink Metalworks supplied the stainless steel grille insert.

Left: This is a fully reworked Corvette LT4 V8 that was stripped, smoothed and detailed with a custom cover for the injection unit, and stainless steel headers.

Opposite: *Street Rodder* magazine staffer Eric Geisert owns this Model A roadster, dubbed California Spyder. Working to a Chip Foose design, the roadster came together slowly over three years, using many of the best shops in So Cal, and featured in a build-up series in the magazine. Acme Custom Cars applied the paint to what was once a rusted desert-dwelling bodyshell. Powered by Ford with an overdrive trans and disc brakes all round, the roadster made its debut on the main floor of the 50th Grand National Roadster Show.

Above: Working to a controversial design by Thom Taylor saw Craig Naff fabricate the body for the first all-aluminum bodied Boyd-built car. Although the "steam iron" front end styling divided opinion, it won the AMBR trophy in 1990 for owner Butch Martino. Martino wanted a narrow streamlined roadster in aluminum, and Boyd's talented craftsmen came up with exactly what he asked for.

Right: The Boydster is Boyd Coddington's personal AMBR winner, after having been responsible for six winners of the trophy for other people. The hand-formed '32-like body came from the talented hands of Marcel DeLay and sons, working to a Chip Foose design. Longtime friend L'il John Buttera machined the three-spoke billet wheels, Gabe Lopez stitching the red leather interior behind a curved windshield.

Left: Attebury Street Rods constructed this '33 with a short wraparound windshield that continues through the doors and tapers off on the tops of the quarter panels, a tilt front hiding a polished Corvette motor. The nacelles behind each headrest are echoed in the hood sides, which also feature custom headlights. Jack Hagemann fabricated the one-piece front, while Sid Chavers stitched the interior, and Colorado Custom supplied the three-spoke wheels.

Right: Joe McPherson's Infinity Flyer couldn't quite hide its DOHC Q-45 V8 motor under the hood, hence the bulges in the side panels. The frameless windshield-equipped roadster was based on a '29A on '32 rails, though plenty of changes were made by Art and Mike Chrisman, and Steve Davis. Tony Nancy upholstered the '94 AMBR winner.

Opposite: Neal East owns this '27T Mocified which runs an aluminum Buick V8 under its three piece hood, connected to a five speed transmission, and Halibrand quick change. The most unusual feature is the underslung chassis at the front, the dropped axle suspended on inverted leaf springs. Cast finish "kidney bean" Halibrand wheels are the finishing touch.

Above: Famed and much respected automotive paint specialist Stan Betz owns this Art Barker hand-crafted roadster pick-up, dubbed 2032. The one-off body and bed sits on a custom chassis, a modular Lincoln MkVIII motor under the alligator-style hood. Glenn Lorton laid on the Betz-mixed paint.

Right: Built for paint manufacturer DuPont, the DuPont Domination had over 2,000 hours invested by Mickey Galloway in the Chevy bodywork alone before it was mounted on the Colorado Custom wheel-adorned high-tech, independently suspended chassis from Dominator Motorsports.

Below: Well known custom builder Rick Dore unveiled this gorgeous '36 in 1998, incorporating a '40 Packard grille and '37 Buick headlights with reworked hood and side panels, which in turn opened up with unique vents. Starting with a coupe, the roof was removed, the windshield frame chopped, and a Carson top fabricated. A Mustang II IFS and 9in rear were installed on airbags, before the car was shipped to Acme Custom Cars for the bodywork to be modified and readied for the tangerine candy paint.

Above: Northern California rodder Jim Stroupe owns this T Modified powered by a rare four pot Lemco motor. Plenty of neat touches abound, from the spring perch exiting through the centre of the grille to the early-style implement front tires.

Opposite: Is it a new car or been around for decades? It was hard to tell with the quality of nostalgia rods by the end of the decade, but this Vertex magneto and SCoT-blown equipped flathead-powered '32 cabriolet fits in with then-current trends.

Right: This smooth '34 roadster exemplifies late '90s rodding, from its vanilla paint and burgundy roof to the billet wheels and DuVall windshield.

Right: The BDS injector stacks are what first get your attention, and are what prompted owner Chuck McCoy to name his roadster Stacks. The tubbed Deuce from Washington state runs a Kugel custom IFS, and has a Mark Williams nodular 9in axle, with a neat roll hoop behind the driver, and a cast So Cal Speed Shop windshield.

Opposite: Based on the design of a Brogie roadster, Martin Curbishley's '27T does double duty competing in both Super Gas and Super Comp, proving very competitive and relatively maintenance-free—firstly with a big-block Ford, and latterly with a big Chevy for power.

Left: The sheetmetal on this '34 Ford woodie has been altered so the hood opens alligator-style, and reflects the smoothy trend, yet the wood is all done in original style, including screens instead of glass in the rear side windows. Despite the apparent mix of styles, the overall concept really works!

Right: Compare these traditional fading flames with blue pinstriping to the tribal style on the right. Both styles and variants in between have their place at the beginning of the 21st century, in an era where seemingly "anything goes" in street rodding. It's surely the best time ever to build a street rod, being able to pick a favorite look or style from the past 50-plus years, or trying something completely new.

Opposite: M2000 was built for *Street Rodder* magazine's fifth Road Tour, to showcase aftermarket street rod manufacturers' products at NSRA events throughout the year. It was also conceived as a continuation of Tom McMullen's roadster series, but as a modern representation rather than another clone. Billet Specialties wheels, a Downs Manufacturing body, and Heidt's Superide front and rear suspensions were just part of the package.

Classic Profile: *1940 WILLYS SEDAN*

Shane Weckerly is shop foreman at So Cal Speed Shop, and this is his personal transport, a '40 Willys sedan that he rescued when he was 19, then spent ten years two-dooring and turning it into the blown, injected, and flamed street rod seen here. Beck Racing Engines in Phoenix, Arizona handled the machine work on the '57 392ci Chrysler hemi, Weckerly adding a 6-71 Mooneyham blower, and Enderle bugcatcher injection. Out the back 14x15in Real Wheels are matched by spindle-mount Halibrands up front, while the paint was applied by John Carambia—the flames then added by Dennis Ricklefs.

A ten point NHRA-legal rollcage dominates the Ron Mangus-stitched interior should Weckerly feel the need to exercise his sedan at the drags.

Right: The zoomie headers poking out from beneath the rear of the front fenders do contain small baffles, but blown hemi's aren't the quietest of engines, and this one's LOUD! The louvers in the hood remove unwanted heat, assisting the Ron Davis-built aluminum radiator and twin electric fans. Weckerly built his own frame from 2x4in box section, utilizing parts of the original side rails, and added an adjustable four link at the rear, and a Mustang II front crossmember, filled and smoothed before the frame was powder coated black.

Above: Beneath that 6-71 Mooneyham blower and Enderle bug catcher injection system is a 1957 vintage Chrysler A-1 hemi V8. Bored 40 thou over stock and converted to four bolt mains it runs 8:1 JE pistons, and an Engle roller cam. The ported and polished heads contain Donovan stainless steel valves, rocker arms, gear drive, and valve covers with a Mike Kuhl water pump keeping coolant flowing. A 727 Torqueflite trans moves the power down to a heavy duty 9in axle with a Strange spool, and Moser 35 spline shafts.

Below: Coast to Coast produce these slippery '39 Ford based bodies which save a ton of work for those wanting a fat fendered smoothy—just requiring preparation and paint instead of months of metalwork. Topped of with a Carson-style top you can't deny they have "presence."

Opposite: A supercharged big block hauls this prize-winning Pro Street '32 Vicky around in fine style, massive Convo-Pro wheels, and matching rubber filling the rear fenders and intruding well into the bodywork, necessitating new inner fenderwells or "wheel tubs" for clearance.

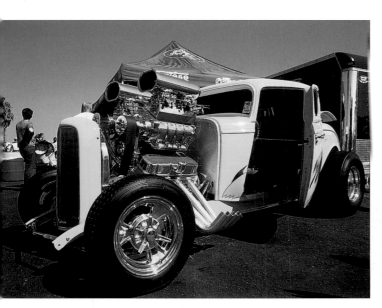

Left: Good to see overkill was still very much alive in the '90s, as evidenced by this twin blown big-block, zoomie headered '32 three window spotted in Florida. If it's a driver there's a heap of money tied up in that motor—if not it probably contains no internals and the blowers could be nicely polished fakes.

Opposite: The great thing about nostalgia rodding in the '90s is that you can put together the most outlandish rod you could wish for. Adrian Smith's A coupe is channeled to death, with a chassis heavily Z'd front and rear, six carbed small block, and a removable padded roof insert.

Right: Large headlights, a drilled visor, and lakes headers poking out over the front fenders give this '28 A Tudor attitude. The green accents continue inside with green metalflake seats and upholstery.

Left: Want a woody? There are a few specialists across the United States who can build a woody from scratch, probably the best known being Wood 'n' Carr in California, and Hercules Motor Company in Florida. Though Hercules specializes in '33 and '34 woodies, all sorts of wagons can be found frequenting their shop on open days, such as this rodded Model A woody.

Right: Polished 20in American Racing Torq Thrust IIs grace each corner of Keith Atkinson's '32, the blue flames matching the blue leather interior. Though not visible here, the flames are duplicated on the inside of the hood.

Left: This lavender T roadster is based on a '27 tub, once the front half of a Touring body, though these days more likely to be a new fiberglass version. Chrome reverse rims and whitewall crossplies lend a 1960s feel, aided by the aluminum Buick V8 and louvered chrome air cleaner.

Right: The mid to late '90s saw a sharp increase in the number of rods and car clubs among the younger crowd, mainly in southern California. The Shifters from Orange County were among the first clubs with nostalgic rods, though in very short order the cars became wackier and crazier in style, almost caricatures of their owners' ideas of what constituted a hot rod. Love 'em or hate 'em, you couldn't ignore 'em!

Opposite: Bob Rydell's 2002 Ridler Award-winning '35 Chevrolet sedan is rolling sculpture at its very finest. Created by the Foose Design team, the two door is absolute perfection, blending countless modifications along with subtle colors.

Above: A '34 with a twist. This is a fiberglass body style manufactured in England and called a Sport Saloon (saloon being the English equivalent of a sedan). It gives the benefit of a rear seat to any rodders who really lust after a coupe, but have the restriction of a small family.

Left: Wayne Streams took a '46 Chevy pick-up, left the body stock apart from a rolled rear pan and slammed it way down over big-inch billet wheels. With a new chromed grille and lilac paint, the once ugly truck became anything but! The running gear was updated, keeping it in the family, with a Chevy small-block under the four piece center-hinged hood.

Above: It shouldn't be forgotten that this hobby is supposed to be about having fun with cars, which is exactly what these three are doing. This traditional-look A on B rails is powered by a Pinto four banger for economic fun, and if the rumble of a V8 isn't that important to you it provides just as much fun at a fraction of the cost.

Left: In the latter half of the '90s air bag suspension began to prove immensely popular, mainly because there's simply no other way to get a car this low and still drive it. With an on-board compressor the air bags can be inflated to raise this '35 coupe to a safe driving height, then deflated again to drop it on the ground when parked.

Opposite: Orange flames brighten up the front of this Pro Street '38 Willys pick-up. The bull nosed front was changed slightly in '39, again in '40, and then yet again for '41—most recognize the front end as being a Willys, with a single grille below the hood in the front panel.

Above: Heavily channeled over a Z'd A frame, Shifters member Mark Idzardi's '28 Roadster pick-up employs a severely chopped windshield with a roof that's hinged at the rear for access. The abbreviated pick-up bed is almost completely filled by the gas tank, feeding the sextet of carbs on the Chevy small block.

Right: Is it a rod or a custom? This '36 qualifies as both. Low and top chopped with rounded door tops says it's a custom; hoodless with a small block, white firewall, and red primer with whitewalls on red steels says it's a hot rod. Whatever your preference, it's cool rod run transportation if this style of car lights your fire.

Below: Kevan Sledge's '24 turtle deck T has been seen in many different guises since it first appeared in 1994. Starting off black with whitewall piecrust slicks on red steels, it progressed through the stage seen here, then orange with four carbs on the '49 Caddy motor, before reappearing in red with wire front wheels, full black interior, and high exhausts terminating at the rear of the doors. The lack of front brakes has always been a constant though, as has the rest of the running gear—each image change more cosmetic than structural.

Classic Profile: FLAMED '40 COUPE

A homage to high school hot rods of the '60s, yet definitely a product of the '90s, Chuck de Heras' '40 Ford coupe is about as cool as they come. Put together at So Cal Speed Shop, starting with a cherry Deluxe coupe, this flamed '40 has received its share of subtle body mods, including a recessed firewall to make space for the huge Mopar Performance 426ci hemi engine. Wanting that mid-'60s high school drag coupe look, Hilborn and BDS were consulted to come up with a nostalgic-appearing yet electronically managed fuel injection system, a one-off nose piece instead of a hood showing off the powerplant in all its glory.

Right: From the custom nerf bar and blanked header pipe to the reworked drip rails and sunken license plate, there's a bunch of subtle bodywork, all eclipsed by the White pinstriped Dennis Rickleffs-applied flames.

Above: That's 426in of Dick Landy-built Mopar Performance hemi squeezed into the engine bay, topped by a Hilborn/EDS electronic fuel injection system that appears nostalgic but has up-to-the-minute performance. The white-firewall-mounted brake master cylinder helps to reinforce the '60s hot rod image. A Hays clutch links the hemi to a Jericho four speed.

Right: A narrowed Thunderbird dash now lives inside the coupe with the trim panels extending on to the doors. together with a T-bird column and '57 Ford steering wheel Ron Mangus stitched the orange and white tuck 'n' roll, while there's a chrome roll bar behind the bench seat.

Above: Paul Atkins' 2000 Ridler Award winner featured incredible attention to detail. Big inch polished five spokes were mounted with motorcycle tires on the front for a funky appearance, while the underside of the Speedstar '33 Ford body and the chassis received as much attention as the top.

Opposite: Roy Brizio Street Rods was responsible for Al Engel's '32 Ford Imperial roadster, a rod featuring many subtle mods.The '32 Chrysler grille, and E&J headlights give the front end a much earlier look than a regular '32 Ford, while the 16in steel wheels shod with Chrysler caps help, too.

Below: With no gimmicks, overkill or cartoonish elements, this '28 on '32 rails is what a lot of early hot rods looked like back in the '40s, though this is a modern version. The flathead V8 is stock with the exception of a set of headers, and the Model A roadster body still wears door handles and a gas cap for the cowl-mounted tank. In fact, the only part out of sync is the too-chopped windshield.

Right: Sure it's bodily stock, but a '36 Ford three window coupe is about near-perfect as it came from the factory. This example has a painted windshield frame and grille insert but that's about it for body mods. The running gear is another matter however, the stance giving away the fact that this coupe is a '90s street rod, with performance and comfort to match.

Left: Early style flames that evoke memories of those painted by Von Dutch adorn this '28 Ford roadster pick-up with '32 grille shell. From San Diego, the channeled truck with shortened bed is owned by a member of the Deacons club—the goings-on inside the Tri-power-fed small-block Chevy monitored via gauges in a rare wide Stewart Warner gauge panel.

Opposite: Graphics, particularly flames, seem to have made a comeback in the new century, with ideas such as the "torn flag" graphics in this Anglia gaining in popularity. With cutaway hood sides to show off the small block, this Anglia has been chopped, and had widened fenders added among many other bodymods.

Classic Profile: *PEACHY '32*

If this roadster were described by just listing the parts—blown Ardun headed flathead, full fendered smooth body, lakes style headers and wire wheels—it doesn't sound as though it would work as a whole, but in the flesh it's proof of what can be achieved by careful selection of parts and mixing of styles. It's this mixing of styles—that's very easy to get wrong but difficult to get spot on as here—that is happening in the hobby at the start of the new millennium, and what makes building a hot rod or street rod right now so exciting.

Right: Detailed chromed and polished to the max, old Henry's little sidevalve V8 never looked so good! The peach-painted block is almost completely hidden under the Ardun heads and polished 6-71 supercharger, the megaphone headers only just clearing the fender and firewall. Discoloration of the headers proves that it's a runner, too.

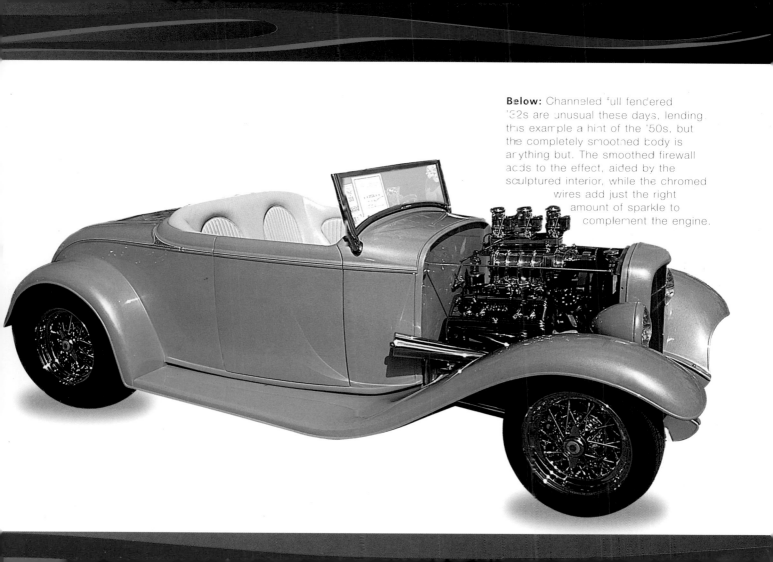

Below: Channeled full fendered '32s are unusual these days, lending this example a hint of the '50s, but the completely smoothed body is anything but. The smoothed firewall adds to the effect, aided by the sculptured interior, while the chromed wires add just the right amount of sparkle to complement the engine.

INDEX

Photo Credits

The publishers would like to thank the following people for contributing their photographs for this book:
Mike Key supplied the majority of pictures for this book—all those not listed below; Bo Bertilsson (4, 6, 30L, 36L&R, 46L&R, 50L, 54, 59R, 65R, 68, 70, 72, 74, 75T, 80R, 92–3, 102–103, 108–109, 110–11, 115, 143, 223, 260L, 266–7, 301L, 356, 357L; Kev Elliott (66, 82T, 83, 95, 120–1, 288L, 320R, 324L, 377R, 382, 384–5, 390L, 392); Mark Gredzinski (367R); Chuck Vranas (82M, 86R, 87R, 88, 89L, 91, 97R, 104–105, 107L, 117, 118–19, 122L, 125L&R, 132L, 172L, 336R, 378, 388, 389. (L=Left; M=Middle; R=Right; T=Top of the page in question.)